DERMOT MAC MORROGH,

OR

THE CONQUEST OF IRELAND.

AN

HISTORICAL TALE OF THE TWELFTH CENTURY.

IN

FOUR CANTOS.

BY JOHN QUINCY ADAMS.

THIRD EDITION.

Quarum autem rerum ante nostros oculos contidiana documenta versantur, licet genere non minus mirabili, ipsa tamen assiduitate vilescunt. *Giraldus Cambrensis*, *Expugnatio Hiberniæ*, *Sive Historia Vaticinalis.*

COLUMBUS, OHIO:

PUBLISHED BY ISAAC N. WHITING.

1849.

Entered according to Act of Congress in the year 1832,
BY MELVIN LORD,
in the Clerk's Office of the District Court of the District of Massachusetts.

DEDICATION AND PREFACE.

TO MY COUNTRYMEN AND READERS.

History, it hath been said, is Philosophy, teaching by example. This aphorism has made a greater fortune in the world than it deserves. The *examples* which history presents to the contemplation of mankind, if they teach any philosophy at all, it is that of the philosopher Apemantus in Shakspeare's Timon of Athens. To test this truth I would ask the young men and women of my native country, who may charge an idle evening with the perusal of the *History* which I now dedicate to them, what sort of philosophy would be taught by the *example* of Henry the Second of England, or of Dermot Mac Morrogh, king of Leinster, which resulted in the conquest of Ireland by the English monarch.

History, as it should be written and read, is the school of morals, teaching sometimes by example, but much more frequently by admonition. It is a narrative of a few prosperous voyages and multitudes of shipwrecks. But how *is* history written? How is history read? David Hume passes for a *philosophical* historian; and he is much celebrated for the interest which he infuses into his narrative, and for his skill and discernment in the delineation of characters. Now listen to his account of the conquest of Ireland by the murderer of Becket, and then mark the character which he gives of the man.

The following is his summary of the conquest of Ireland:

"Besides many small tribes, there were, in the age of Henry II. five principal sovereignties in the island, Munster, Leinster, Meath, Ulster, and Connaught: and as it had been usual for the one or the other of these to take the lead in their wars, there was commonly some prince, who seemed for the time, to act as monarch of Ireland. Roderick O'Conner, king of Connaught, was then advanced to this dignity; but his government, ill obeyed, even within his own territory, could not unite the people in any measures, either for the establishment of order, or for defence against foreigners. The ambition of Henry had, very early in his reign, been moved, by the prospect of these advantages, to attempt the subjecting of Ireland; and a pretence was only wanting to invade a people, who, being always confined to their own Island, had never given any reason of complaint to any of their neighbors. For this purpose, he had recourse to Rome, which assumed a right to dispose of kingdoms and empires; and, not foreseeing the dangerous disputes, which he was one day to maintain with that See, he helped, for present, or rather for an imaginary convenience, to give sanction to claims, which were now become dangerous to all sovereigns. Adrian III. who then filled the papal chair, was by birth an Englishman; and being on that account the more disposed to oblige Henry, he was easily persuaded to act as master of the world, and to make, without any hazard or expense, the acquisition of a great island, to his spiritual jurisdiction. The Irish had, by precedent missions from the Britons, been imperfectly converted to Christianity; and, what the pope regarded as the surest mark of their imperfect conversion, they followed the doctrines of their first teachers, and had never acknowledged any subjection to the See of Rome. Adrian, therefore, in the year 1156, issued a bull in favor of Henry; in which, after premising that this prince had ever shown an anxious care to enlarge the church of God on earth, and to increase the number of his saints and elect in Heaven, he represents his design of subduing Ireland as derived from the same pious motives: he considers his care of previously applying for the apostolic sanction as a sure earnest of success and victory; and having established it as a point incontestable, that all Christian kingdoms belong to the patrimony of St. Peter, he acknowledges it to be his own duty to sow among them the seeds of the gospel, which might, in the last day, fructify to their eternal salvation: he exhorts the king to invade Ireland, in order to extirpate the vice and wickedness of the natives, and oblige them to pay, yearly, from every house, a penny to the See of Rome; he gives him entire right and authority over the island, commands all the inhabitants to obey him as their sovereign, and invests with full power, all such godly instruments, as he should think proper to employ in an enterprise thus calculated for the glory of God, and the salvation of the souls of men. Henry, though armed with this authority, did not immediately put his design in execution; but, being detained by more interesting business on the continent, waited for a favorable opportunity of invading Ireland.

"Dermot Mac Morrogh, king of Leinster, had, by his licentious tyranny, rendered himself odious to his subjects, who seized with alacrity the first occasion that offered of throwing off the yoke, which was become grievous and oppressive to them. This prince had formed a design on Dovergilda, wife of Ororic, prince of Breffny; and taking advantage of her husband's absence, who being obliged to visit a distant part of his territory, had left his wife secure, as he thought, in an island surrounded by a bog, he suddenly invaded the place, and carried off the princess. This exploit, though usual among the Irish, and rather deemed a proof of gallantry and spirit, provoked the resentment of the husband, who, having collected forces, and being strengthened by the alliance of Roderic, king of Connaught, invaded the dominions of Dermot, and expelled him his kingdom. The exiled prince had recourse to Henry, who was at this time in Guienne, craved his assistance in restoring him to his sovereignty, and offered on that event, to hold his kingdom in vassalage under the crown of England. Henry, whose views were already turned towards making acquisitions in Ireland, readily accepted the offer; but, being at that time embarrassed by the rebellions of his French subjects, as well as by his disputes with the See of Rome, he declined, for the present, embarking in the enterprise, and gave Dermot no further assistance than letters patent, by which he empowered all his subjects to aid the Irish prince in the recovery of his dominions. Dermot supported by this authority, came to Bristol; and after endeavoring, though for some time in vain, to engage adventurers in the enterprise, he at last formed a treaty with Richard, surnamed Strongbow, Earl of Strigul. This nobleman, who was of the illustrious house of Clare, had impaired his fortune by expensive pleasures; and being ready for any desperate undertaking, he promised assistance to Dermot, on condition that he should espouse Eva, daughter of that prince, and be declared heir to all his dominions. While Richard was assembling his succors, Dermot went into Wales; and meeting with Robert Fitzt-Stephen, constable of Abertivi, and Maurice Fitz-Gerald, he also engaged them in his service, and obtained their promise of invading Ireland. Being now assured of succor, he returned privately to his own state; and lurking in the monastery of Fernes, which he had founded, (for this ruffian was also a founder of monasteries) he prepared every thing for the reception of his English allies.

"The troops of Fitz-Stephen were first ready. That gentleman landed in Ireland, with thirty knights, sixty esquires, and three hundred archers; but this small body, being brave men, not unacquainted with discipline, and completely armed, a thing almost unknown in Ireland, struck a great terror into the barbarous inhabitants, and seemed to menace them with some signal revolution. The conjunction of Maurice de Pendergast, who, about the same time, brought over ten knights and sixty archers, enabled Fitz-Stephen to attempt the siege of Wexford a town inhabited by the Danes; and after gaining an advantage, he made himself master of the place. Soon after Fitz-Gerald arrived with ten knights, thirty esquires; and being joined by the former adventurers, composed a force, which nothing in Ireland was able to withstand. Roderic, the chief monarch of the island, was foiled in different actions;—the prince of Ossory was obliged to submit, and give hostages for his peaceable behaviour; and Dermot, not content with being restored to his kingdom of Leinster, projected the dethroning of Roderic, and aspired to the sole dominion over the Irish.

"In prosecution of these views, he sent over a messenger to the earl of Strigul, challenging the performance of his promise, and displaying the mighty advantages, which might now be reaped, by a reinforcement of warlike troops, from England. Richard, not satisfied with the general allowance given by Henry to all his subjects, went to that prince, then in Normandy; and, having obtained a cold or ambiguous permission, prepared himself for the execution of his designs. He first sent over Raymond, one of his retinue, with ten knights and seventy archers, who, landing near Waterford, defeated a body of three thousand Irish, that had ventured to attack him; and as Richard himself, who brought over two hundred horse, and a body of archers, joined, a few days after, the victorious English, they made themselves masters of Waterford, and proceeded to Dublin, which was taken by assault. Roderic, in revenge, cut off the head of Dermot's natural son, who had been left as an hostage in his hands; and Richard, marrying Eva, became, soon after, by the death of Dermot, master of the kingdom of Leinster, and prepared to extend his authority over all Ireland. Roderic and the other Irish princes were alarmed at the danger; and combining together, besieged Dublin, with an army of thirty thousand men: but earl Richard, making a sudden sally, at the head of ninety knights, with their followers, put this numerous army to rout, chased them off the field, and pursued them with great slaughter. None, in Ireland, now dared to oppose themselves to the English.

"Henry, jealous for the progress made by his own subjects, sent orders to recall all the English, and he made preparations to attack Ireland in person: but Richard, and the other adventurers, found means to appease him, by making him the most humble submissions, and offering to hold all the acquisitions in vassalage to his crown. That monarch landed in Ireland, at the head of five hundred knights, besides other soldiers: he found the Irish so dispirited by their late misfortunes, that in a progress, which he made through the island, he had no other occupation than to receive the homage of his new subjects. He left most of the Irish chieftains, or princes, in possession of their ancient territories; bestowed some land on the English adventurers, gave earl Richard the commission of seneschal of Ireland: and after a stay of a few months, returned in triumph to England. By these trivial exploits, scarcely worth relating, except for the importance of the consequences, was Ireland subdued, and annexed to the English crown."

And now for the character of the hero who achieved this conquest:

"Thus died, in the fifty-eighth year of his age and thirty-fifth of his reign, the greatest prince of his time, for wisdom, virtue and abilities, and the most powerful, in extent of dominion, of all those who had ever filled the throne of England. His character in private, as well as in public life, is almost without a blemish; and he seems to have possessed every accomplishment, both of body and mind, which makes a man either estimable or amiable. He was of a middle stature, strong and well proportioned; his countenance was lively and engaging; his conversation affable and entertaining; his elocution, easy, persuasive, and ever at command. He loved peace, but possessed both bravery and conduct in war: was provident without timidity; severe in the execution of justice without rigor; and temperate without austerity. He preserved health, and kept himself from corpulency, to which he was somewhat inclined, by an abstemious diet, and by frequent exercise, particularly hunting. When he could enjoy leisure, he recreated himself either in learned conversation, or in reading; and he cultivated his natural talents, by study, above any prince of his time. His affections, as well as his enmities, were warm and durable; and his long experience of the ingratitude and infidelity of men never destroyed the natural sensibility of his temper, which disposed him to friendship and society. His character has been transmitted to us by several writers, who were his contemporaries; and it extremely resembles, in its most remarkable features, that of his maternal grandfather, Henry I. excepting, only that ambition, which was a ruling passion in both, found not, in the first Henry, such unexceptionable means of exerting itself, and pushed that prince into measures, which were both criminal in themselves, and were the cause of farther crimes, from which his grandson's conduct was happily exempted."

So much for Hume's philosophy, teaching by the example of Henry the Second. If there be in the annals of the human race, a transaction of deeper and more melancholy depravity than the conquest of Ireland by Henry the second, it has not fallen under my notice. It would seem as if it could not be accomplished but by a complication of the most odious crimes, public and private. Dermot Mac Morrogh, for insupportable tyranny over his subjects, aggravated by the violation of the most sacred of human ties, the seduction of another's wife, is justly expelled from his kingdom. He immediately repairs to "the greatest prince of his time, for wisdom, virtue and abilities," and sells his country for the price of being restored by the foreign invader to his principality. The English king, to cover the basest of aggressions with the mantle of religion, applies to Pope Adrian the Third, an Englishman, for authority to ravage Ireland with fire and sword, under pretence of reforming the inhabitants, and reducing them to the orthodox faith of paying tribute to the Roman See. This authority Pope Adrian grants him without scruple. You may read in Rapin the *brief* itself. And with this sacrilegious abuse of religion, Henry, reeking with the blood of Becket, and Dermot, the ruffian builder of monasteries, achieve the conquest of Ireland, in vassalage to the crown of England.— And this is the tenure by which Ireland is held as an appendage to the sister island, at the present day.

History, I have said, should be the school of morals. When I first read this part of Hume's history, I was shocked at the careless indifference with which he tells this tale of wickedness and wo; and at the unqualified panegyric which he passes upon the character of Henry the Second— a great man, no doubt, and a hero, but in the estimate of philosophic virtue as mixed a character as has appeared on the checkered scene of human affairs. The history of the conquest of Ireland appeared to me to be full of instruction, by an exhibition of the actions and motives which concurred to effect it. But to bring these into proper relief it was necessary that it should be told again. The period however was remote; the history of Ireland had, by the subjugation of that island, been merged in that of her overshadowing neighbor and mistress, and the conquest of a land, at this day bearing a population of seven millions of souls, had sunk into a mere incident in the annals of England, scarcely known or noticed by the general readers of history. The characters, excepting that of the principal adventurer, Henry Plantagenet were so obscure and mouldering into oblivion, that I doubt whether one in a hundred of my readers will on first seeing my title-page recollect or even know that such a personage as Dermot Mac Morrogh ever existed. To give the story therefore an interest which might invite readers, it appeared to me advisable to present it in the garb of poetry. The subject was well adapted to the composition of an historical tale, and as such I deliver it to the judgment of my country. It is intended also as a moral tale, teaching the citizens of these States of both sexes, the virtues of conjugal fidelity, of genuine piety, and of devotion to their country, by pointing the finger of scorn at the example six hundred years since exhibited, of a country sold to a foreign invader by the joint agency of violated marriage vows, unprincipled ambition, and religious imposture.

JOHN QUINCY ADAMS.

QUINCY, *October* 25, 1832.

NOTICE.

The history of the Conquest of Ireland by Henry the Second, was first written in Latin by Giraldus Cambrensis, a monk who attended Prince John, son of Henry, into Ireland. The Irish names of that age are differently written and spelt, by different writers. I have adopted the names of Dermot Mac Morrogh, of Dovergilda, and of Ororik, from Hume, the historian I presume most familiarly known to general readers. In Leland's History of Ireland they are called Dermod Mac Murshad, Dervorghal, and Tiernan O'Ruarc. Lord Lyttleton, in his History of Henry the second, calls them "Dermod Mac Murogh, or as some call him, Mac Murchad, Ternan O'Ruark, and Devorgalla." Others spell the name of the prince of Breffny, O'Rourke. It is sometimes of two syllables and sometimes of three, a matter of some moment in the composition of verse.

DERMOT MAC MORROGH.

CANTO I.

THE ELOPEMENT.

I.

I sing of Dermot, Erin's early pride;
  The pious patriot of Emerald strand;
The first deliverer, for a stol'n bride
  Who sold to Albian's king his native land.
But—countrymen of mine, let wo betide
  The man who thinks of aught but what's in hand.
What I shall tell you, happen'd you must know,
  Beyond the seas, six hundred years ago.

II.

'Tis strange how often readers will indulge
  Their wits a mystic meaning to discover;
Secrets ne'er dreamt of by the bard divulge,
  And where he shoots a duck, will find a plover:
Satiric shafts from every line promulge,
  Detect a tyrant, when he draws a lover:
Nay, so intent his hidden thoughts to see,
  Cry, if he paint a scoundrel—"That means me."

III.

'Tis human nature. In old Roman days,
  When that sweet Mantuan minstrel tuned his lyre;
Sung how Æneas from the Trojan blaze
  On his broad shoulders bore away his sire;
Yet scrupled not, with vilest arts, to raise
  In Tyrian Dido's veins, unhallow'd fire:
Debauch'd her; left her, 'whelm'd with scorn and shame,
  By self-combustion to redeem her fame.

IV.

The Roman delvers straight began to pry
  Into the courtier minstrel's ull intent:
Troy's fall, Rome's rise, they ken'd with half an eye,
  Was but the outward mask of what he meant:
His patron prince with oil of fools to ply,
  They soon discover'd was the poet's bent:
The good Æneas was a wisp of straw;
  Augustus Cæsar was the man they saw.

V.

And so for sixteen hundred years and more
  That wiley knave for Virgil's hero pass'd;
Till Father Hardouin, vers'd in classic lore,
  To find another clue about him cast:
And, wont in legendary lies to pore,
  He delv'd, and delv'd, and delv'd, and found at last,
That Virgil's Æneid was a monkish tale,
  In verse, our saviour's passion to unveil.

VI.

Poor Salignac ! how hard a fate was thine ;
Thy pupil, heir apparent to a throne,
Thou drew'st the moral gem from Homer's mine,
And mad'st the Grecian Muses all thy own.
To teach him wisdom with a voice divine ;
This was thy noble purpose, this alone :
But when thou painted'st court and courtesan,
They said 't was Louis and his Montespan.

VII.

Against all this, I enter my protest :
Dermot Mac Morrogh shows my hero's face ;
Nor will I, in earnest or in jest,
Permit another to usurp his place ;
And give me leave to say that I know best
My own intentions in the lines I trace ;
Let no man therefore draw aside the screen,
And say 't is any other that I mean.

VIII.

Fair Albion's Isle, 't is known to all of you,
Once by a Norman bastard was subdued:
And well dispos'd was that same hero too
On Erin's Isle his sceptre to obtrude.
She never had offended him, 't is true :
She pleas'd him : was so near : her sons were rude ;
Not half so warlike as *his* Norman knights :
What hero ever thought of people's rights?

IX.

Keen was King William's relish, all his life
For the bright beauties of the verdant Isle:
But England, Scotland, Wales, incessant strife,
The conqueror's doom, consum'd his days the while.
His son, the scholar, though less long his knife,
Beheld the beauty too with wistful smile:
Heroes and scholars have alike their lease:
Still Erin bloom'd in loveliness and peace.

X.

But ages pass, and human lusts remain;
And nature's charms from age to age abide:
Britannia's throne no monarch could attain,
But *there* was tempting Erin at her side.
The second Henry came in turn to reign:
He too beheld her in her virgin pride;
And fiercely bent to rifle all her charms,
Implor'd the Pope to consecrate his arms,

XI.

For Erin fair, it was by all agreed,
Did to his Holiness the Pope belong;
Nor was there mortal dar'd dispute the creed;
St. Peter's keys had made the title strong.
And Constantine had granted him by deed
All Islands—so 't was broad as it was long.
Of both the grants she fell within the scope—
Fee simple to his Holiness the Pope.

XII.

But what was Henry's reason or pretence,
Presented to the Holy Father's view ?
What plea of law, what ray of common sense,
With fire and sword fair Erin to subdue ?
'Twas holy zeal, 'twas piety intense,
To curb and civilize the barbarous crew*;
Make them keep Easter on the proper day ;
And Peter's pence to Christ's vicegerent pay.

XIII.

Pope Adrian was, himself, a Briton born ;
Such soft persuasion how could he resist ?
How treat his liege lord's filial love with scorn ?
(His foot, for Henry, John of Sarum kiss'd.)
The holy zeal of Henry fill'd the horn
Of fame ; so John of Sarum was dismiss'd :
Charg'd with the bull, to ravage Erin's land,
And yield her beauties to the spoiler's hand.

XIV.

Divine Religion ! bliss of man below,
Thou link of union between earth and skies ;
Nurse of our virtue, solace of our wo ;
Lore of the learned, wisdom of the wise.
Thou from whose fountain, streams perennial flow,
Of prayer sincere, and praise and penance rise.
Oh ! how canst thou behold such deeds of shame,
Such crimes accurst, committed in thy name?

XV.

But good and evil rule on earth by turns;
Vice often borrows virtue's brightest hue:
And nought but God's all seeing eye discerns
Within the heart, the counterfeit and true;
On crime's high altar hallow'd incense burns;
Ruffians can pray,—ay, and build churches too;
And tyrants, pouring vows, from lips unchaste,
Rise but to lay God's fair creation waste.

XVI.

And such was Henry; such was Leinster's lord;
Dermot, whose fame in this my lay survives—
Men who could bind in desperate accord
Religious fervor, with licentious lives.
Could dare at once to tempt with vows abhorr'd
The Lord of glory, and their neighbors' wives:
And thought by rearing convents to atone
For rapine, lust and murder on the throne.

XVII.

Dermot Mac Morrogh cast lascivious eyes
On Dovergilda, wife of Breffny's Prince.
This need not startle readers with surprise;
Such things have happen'd both before and since.
"Thou shalt not covet," precept good and wise,
From Sinai sent, makes human passions wince;
The knee can bend, the tongue devoutly pray,
And yet the heart, the foulest vices sway.

XVIII.

This Breffny's Prince, (Ororik was his name,)
Was Dermot's friend, and had a lovely wife;
Possess'd of charms well suited to inflame
The rudest hearts with rivalry and strife—
Young, lively, tender, thoughtless was the dame;
Like many a damsel in the dawn of life:
And thought, though link'd in wedlock to her spouse,
More of her beauty, than her marriage vows.

XIX.

Her lord, and Dermot, as I said before,
Were friends, and pass'd in harmony their days—
Together hunted oft the tusky boar;
Together often join'd the festal blaze;
Their sports were common, common was their store,
Could friendship's revels dark suspicions raise?
The fury slumber'd in Ororik's soul,
Till the dear friend his wife's affections stole.

XX.

And hence a feud between the chiefs arose:
And border war, and desolation's hand;
With midnight fire the humble cottage glows,
And fear and ruin stalk along the land.
Still the old moral my new fable shows;
Of flames and slaughter, woman is the brand;
Oh, shield him, Heaven! whatever fate impend;
Shield, from the perjur'd wife, and faithless friend.

XXI.

Ororik's wife, with Dermot was in league,
False to her husband, traitress to his bed:
For two long years she spun the base intrigue
Of which a chambermaid still held the thread.
A dext'rous valet too, whose name was Teague,
With secret finger smooth'd his master's head—
All join'd to plant Ororik's path with thorns;
And on his royal brow, a pair of horns.

XXII.

Ororik was a warrior bold and brave,
Such as fair Erin in all ages breeds;
Unconscious that the earth can bear a knave:
For fragrant flowers, mistaking rankest weeds:—
Who would not lie, their very souls to save;
See no distinction between words and deeds:
And, ever judging by themselves of others,
Behold in all mankind a band of brothers.

XXIII.

But Dermot's heart in quite another mould
Was form'd—faith, virtue, were to him unknown:
Brave was he as Ororik, and as bold;
But truth and justice never reach'd his throne.
The fiercest passions still his breast control'd;
Reckless of feelings other than his own—
His word, his bond, his oath, nay, altogether,
Weigh'd in his blance, lighter than a feather.

XXIV.

As Dermot by his subjects was detested,
As tyrants like him never fail to be—
Their rights he spurn'd, their privileges wrested;
Their ruin'd daughters fill'd his heart with glee;
Not one dependent was left unmolested,
Till Leinster wither'd like a blasted tree.
And whereso'er one look his eye had cast,
It seem'd as if consuming fire had past.

XXV.

Ororik, as it chanc'd, was call'd one day
To view a distant part of his domains:
And fearing lest his wife should go astray,
How to secure her puzzled much his brains;
He had an island where a castle lay,
Between two rivers and surrounding plains—
With deep ravines dividing every part;
And bogs as bottomless as Dermot's heart.

XXVI.

And there he left his Dovergilda fair,
In charge of Teague; his tried and trusty knave—
For Teague, in concert with the lawless pair,
And his own faithful service to engrave
In his lord's breast, had warn'd him to beware
Of Dermot, dissolute no less than brave:
And Agnes too, the chambermaid so sly,
Was left, upon her mistress as a spy.

XXVII.

Thus guarded, well the reader may suppose,
   What shelter Doverglda's virtue found,
In that same island which her husband chose,
   With bogs, ravines and rivers all around.
Such obstacles were likely to oppose
   To Dermot no insuperable mound :
Alas ! what chain, what fetters e'er could bind,
The wilful workings of a woman's mind.

XXVIII.

When darkness o'er the world her dews had shed,
   And death-like slumber weigh'd upon the land :
With twenty chosen horsemen, Dermot sped ;
   Plung'd in the stream and gain'd the adverse strand ;
Along the river's banks, the troopers spread :
   There Teague awaited him with cap in hand ;
Disclos'd the secret path-way from the shore,
Perfidious pilot, to the castle's door.

XXIX.

And Agnes the discreet, was watching here—
   Lurking beneath the sable veil of night—
Without the castle walls the draw-bridge near,
   Her faithless bosom trembling with affright.
'Twas not detected guilt that caus'd her fear :
   'Twas fancy's conscience, t'was the goblin spirit :
And not a leaf could rustle in the breeze,
But Agnes heard a ghost among the trees.

XXX.

She listens—(all her nerves with tremor thrill;—)
Nor the lone nightingale's soft descant heeds.
Hark! she has caught the signal whistle shrill:
And now, the distant trampling of the steeds.
No more she trembles, though the night is chill;
No more invokes the saints, nor tells her beads:
Across the moat, King Dermot's band she saw;
And straight, her gentle hands let down the draw.

XXXI.

Dermot dismounted at the castle gate,
And to a page, resign'd his courser's rein,
Enjoining on his troopers there to wait
His quick return, and on their steeds remain.
Then tripp'd across the bridge with soul elate,
And purpose fell, and palpitating vein—
There meets the chamber-maid his steps to guide
Up the long winding staircase to the bride.

XXXII.

And there he found asleep his lovely prize;
Or at the least he found her there in bed;
It might be she expected a surprise,
And for true slumber clos'd her eyes instead.
And now 't is Agnes calls "Oh, lady! rise!"
And shakes the pillow at her couch's head!
"Oh lady! lady! from thy sleep awaken!
Wretch that I am! the castle has been taken!'

XXXIII.

And up she started, and beheld the chief,
By the pale lamp that glimmer'd in the room;
And feebly shriek'd and wrung her hands for grief;
And cried, "Alas, how wretched is my doom!"
"Oh! lady fair—my errand here is brief,"
Cried Dermot—"fear not; nor indulge in gloom;
"'Tis only, falling on my bended knee
Thy favor to implore······to go with me."

XXXIV.

The lady thought it was a strange request;
And so do I; and so perchance do you.
But then we cannot always choose the best:
Sometimes we have a choice of evils too.
The kneeling prince who waited her behest,
Had in his hand a naked sword, 't is true:
Suppose she should deny his suit—"of course,"
Thought she—"he surely will resort to force."

XXXV.

"Oh! Agnes! Agnes! what will people say,"—
Exclaim'd the lady with a briny flood;
"If from the castle, while my lord's away
I should depart; though to save shedding blood?"
"But wherefore did my lord at home not stay?"
Said the shrewd maid—"why leave us here in mud?
Two women! sure, he never could surmise,
With Teague, could guard his castle from surprise!

XXXVI.

"And where he went, is doubtless known to him;
And others too might guess if they should dare.
The Lady Ursula is tall and slim;
And you have often heard him call her fair—
Though to *my* judgment 't were a wondrous whim,
With YOU, that awkward spindle to compare—
I never saw her; but I've heard them say
Her face is freckled, and her eyes are gray."

XXXVII.

"Fie! Agnes," quoth the lady—"say not so—
My lord, that lady does indeed admire
More than she merits. But, Lord Dermot, go—
To the next chamber, while I dress, retire—
The holy Virgin, and the angles know,
Against my will I yield to your desire:
I see too clearly we are in your power:
Withdraw—and come again in half an hour."

XXXVIII.

And Dermot started, instant from his knee—
And to the antechamber straight withdrew—
"What charms"—said then the dame—"my lord could see
In that same Ursula, I never knew—
'Twas true in part, that which was told to thee—
Her face is freckled; but her eyes are blue.
And then her hair is red."—The lady's look
While speaking, her own sable ringlets took.

XXXIX.

"Bring me my mirror, Agnes—and the light!"
  The lamp and mirror Agnes forthwith brought.
"How deadly pale I look!—'t is this vile fright:
  My box of carmine, Anges—where's your thought?
How cruel, thus to be disturb'd at night!"
  And then her cheek the deep vermilion caught—
"My ruby drops and sapphire necklace bring;
My golden bracelets, and my diamond ring."

XL.

Perhaps the curious reader may inquire,
  Why at this moment of her deep distress,
The lady thought so much of her attire,
  And wasted so much time upon her dress?
Was it, a deeper passion to inspire?
  But here, my ignorance I must confess—
Were it not prov'd I scarcely had believ'd it—
I only give the tale as I receiv'd it.

XLI.

But sure it was—the full half hour had fled:
  And she was busied at her toilet still:
For even after she had sprung from bed,
  She tied a ribbon and she smooth'd a frill.
A beaver with black plumes adorn'd her head:
  Agnes the riding-dress had trim'd with skill:
Till Dermot's patience could no longer last—
"Come, lady, come, your half hour is long past."

XLII.

He enter'd, seiz'd her hand, and forth they went—
  He found his troopers at the castle gate.—
But now, remorse the tender conscience rent
  Of that fair lady, in her pride of state.
In tears her soft compassion soon found vent—
  Fain would she have turn'd back—it was too late:
One parting pang with grief her bosom tore,
For nuptial vows—she thought of them no more.

XLIII.

And at the gate a milk white palfry stood;
  Gaily caparison'd, with curb and rein,
Which trusty Teague in foresight had thought good
  To lead forth from the stables, on the plain.
The ladies of that age, 't is understood,
  Excell'd in horsemanship and us'd no wain.
Nor ditch, nor fence, to them a bar presented:
Coaches and chariots were not then invented.

XLIV.

She sprung into the saddle with a bound;
  And Dermot took his station at her side:
His troopers form'd a hollow square around;
  To guard the ravisher and guilty bride.
Quick! quick, they trample o'er again the ground
  Of the same path-way Teague had made them ride;
They shot across the champain like the wind;
While Teague and Agnes follow'd close behind.

XLV.

Arriving at the landing place, they halted,
  Just as the lovely star of morning rose ;
And with mild radiance from her throne exalted
  Arous'd the hinds of labor from repose :
And soon o'er all the firmament blue-vaulted
  The solar ray with brighter splendor glows.
Alas! why shines alike his dazzling flame,
On deeds of glory and on deeds of shame.

XLVI.

Here while they breath'd their steeds, time on them crept:
  But none was lost, for in a winding bay,
Near that same landing, had Ororik kept
  A trim neat boat, and in a cove she lay
For sailing or for fishing all equipp'd ;
  His wife's amusement, on a summer's day ;
To while away the time in busy leisure ;
And now, be sure, it was a boat for pleasure.

XLVII.

Teague and five troopers were at once despatch'd ;
  To find and to the landing fetch the bark :
While all the rest with trusty caution watch'd
  For the frail fair one and her daring spark :
Soon from her moorings was the boat detach'd,
  Brought to the landing at high water mark ?
And cleav'd with guilty freight the rippling tide,
Till safely landed on the adverse side.

XLVIII.

The troopers plung'd into the stream again,
  Their horses' necks, just peering o'er the wave;
Like Amphitrite's shell upon the main,
  The boat between two files the current clave.
His hand entwisting in his courser's mane,
  Clung to his panting sides, each horseman brave;
While dashing, splashing, snorting as they went,
They reach'd the shore, all dripping drench'd and spent.

XLIX.

Reach'd it?—not all—one trooper lost his hold
  Upon the mane; the courser lost his guide:
Plung'd, flounder'd, struggled,—still the current roll'd,
  And dragg'd them downwards with its rapid tide.
With sense bewilder'd sunk the rider bold:
  Entangled in the stirrup: sunk and died.
Sunk with the steed, five paces from the shore:
A bubbling eddy boil'd—they rose no more.

L.

And so it happen'd that this sad disaster,
  Fell out, in presence of this conscious pair--
The trooper's hapless fate scarce mov'd his master;
  But ruffled somewhat more the lady fair;
She wonder'd why the steed could swim no faster,
  She hop'd the wrath of Heaven the rest would spare.
Landed, they drew the body from the stream;
But gone forever was life's fitful dream.

LI.

His comrads buried him upon the spot:
  A parish priest, at hand, the requiem sung:
And Dermot and the lady soon forgot
  The chance which should their consciences have stung.
Not so the wife of him whose luckless lot
  Has here been told—what pangs her bosom wrung,
Vain the attempts to paint!—suffice to say;
Her senses fled forever from that day.

LII.

But Dermot now resum'd the cavalcade—
  The milk-white palfrey in the sail boat came—
Redoubled assiduities display'd
  The prince's anxious wish to please the dame;
And banish from her thoughts the gloomy shade,
  Caus'd by the sad mischance which seal'd their shame.
O'er Leinster's plains they flew in close array,
And reach'd his castle with departing day.

NOTE.

"Mac Morogh is a word compounded of Mac, which is a sonne, and of Morogh, the proper name of a man, and so Mac Morogh is the sonne of Morogh. And this is common to the Irish and Welsh, for they call not anie man by the name of his familie or nation, as is used in England: but by the name of difference given to his father, as in this example: Dermon being Morogh's sonne is called Dermon Mac Morogh. But this name of Mac Morogh is since turned and become the name of a familie or nation."—*Hooker's Translation of Sylvester Giraldus Cambrensis, his vaticinall historie of the Conquest of Ireland. Chap. 1. page 2.*

DERMOT MAC MORROGH.

CANTO II.

THE EXPULSION.

I.

How Dermot with his willing captive past
  The time at Fernes, beseems me not to tell—
A veil before them fain the Muse would cast,
  On deeds dishonest she disdains to dwell.
To her far more delightful is the blast,
  When notes of virtue bid her clarion swell.
And ah, how great the pity that her ear
So seldom can be call'd such sounds to hear.

II.

But let us now to Breffny's prince return;
  The friend deceiv'd—the wedded lord betray'd—
The master cheated—how his cheek must burn,
  Returning, when his castle he survey'd?
How sharp the lesson, that sight made him learn!
  Himself the theme of vulgar fable made:
Deserted, robb'd of all that charm'd his life,
By his own house,—his bosom friend—his wife.

III.

Whoever studies the historic page,
And reads the record of departed time,
Shall find in every realm, in every age,
The same return of error, vice, and crime —
The same dramatic persons on the stage;
Or varied only by the name or clime:
Shall still behold the fair and candid race,
Dupes of the artful, victims of the base.

IV.

And yet, man, coming from his Maker's hand,
Cannot exchange his nature if he would:
The dark and cunning thus must ever stand;
Prone to all evil, and averse to good.
The villain's heart can never loose its brand;
The honest heart can never take a hood:
Oh! must it prove until the judgment day,
That half mankind was born the other's prey?

V.

Yet let not hence, presumption dare to scan
The scope and purpose of Almighty mind;
Or scrutinize with impious doubt the plan
Of wisdom and of goodness still combin'd;
Born from the clod of earth, immortal man
To this poor wretched world is not confined:
Though but in part, this system bounds his view,
There is an eye that looks creation through.

VI.

And if there be a ruler of the skies,
Justice, eternal justice is his law—
And whatsoe'er of justice earth denies,
Angelic hands in Heaven shall mend the flaw.
Rise then, on Hope's seraphic pinions rise!—
From worlds beyond the grave, thy comfort draw:
And deem the wrongs that virtue here sustains,
Proofs that on high a God of justice reigns.

VII.

When first Ororik to his castle came;
And found it rifled, desolate and bare;
His honest heart, but half conceiv'd his shame:
His wife a traitress! False! and yet so fair!
On Dermot's violence he fixed the blame
Alone—and deem'd his darling in despair:
His trusty servants, Agnes, too, and Teague:
Sure THEY could not with Dermot be in league.

VIII.

For Teague had warn'd him to distrust his friend:
A proof undoubted of his honest zeal:
The art of Ororik could not comprehend,
Truth to disclose with purpose to conceal.
He thought a secret never could extend
Beyond an action honor might reveal;
And never dreamt, for truth was still his guide,
That speech was given to man, his thoughts to hide.

IX.

Men of such tempers, when they come to find
  Themselves deceiv'd, into quick passion burst ;
It breeds a wild confusion in the mind ;
  And wo to him who meets their fury first--
Ororik's anger nought on earth could bind :
  He rav'd—he storm'd—himself, his rival curst :
Till maddening rage, subsiding into grief,
Exhausted nature found in tears relief.

X.

He summon'd up his household menials, all :
  From them perchance to ascertain his fate—
The cook, the butler, and the seneschal,
  The stable groom, the porter at the gate--
They come submissive to their master's call.
  "Where is your mistress?"—None of them could state
"Tell me at once—or mark the dungeon Keep!"
None could inform him—they were all asleep.

XI.

For Teague, to set their vigilance at fault,
  Permision from the lady had obtain'd :
The butler's keys had op'd the vintage vault ;
  And merry wassail made them addle-brain'd.
Wine—whiskey—and the liquor made of malt,
  In mingled floods the kitchen floor had stain'd :
Till each with staggering step and aching head,
And hiccough short had slunk away to bed.

XII.

The groom alone, a story had to tell;
  And said that some nights since, say three or four,
Between the midnight and the morning bell,
  He heard strange noises at the stable door.
At first he thought it was some goblin spell:
  But when Teague enter'd, his heart beat no more;
And Teague had taken out the palfrey gay;
Saddled and bridled him, and rode away.

XIII.

"I marvel'd much, what Teague, so late at night
  Could with my lady's palfrey want to do:
But then again I thought it easy quite
  To guess, for there had drinking been, I knew.
And I suppos'd he wish'd, as well he might,
  To cool his fingers with the morning dew:
And so I turn'd about and slept till dawn,
And then first heard my lady was withdrawn."

XIV.

Ororik's heart misgave him as he heard;
  But still a lurking cherish'd hope remain'd.
All was not right at home, he sorely fear'd;
  Yet might his wife's departure be constrain'd.
The facts, against her innocence appear'd;
  But though suspicious, facts might be explain'd.
He hop'd his wife was carried off by force—
And to redeem her fix'd at once his course.

XV.

A herald straight to Leinster's lord he sent,
  Demanding that his wife should be restor'd:
And if denied, declaring his intent
  To ravage all his lands with fire and sword.
The herald came, his time while Dermot spent
  In drunken revels at his castle's board—
"On this good sword," he cried, "is my reliance,
Him and his herald, sent back with defiance."

XVI.

And back the herald to his lord return'd;
  Reporting how his message had been slighted—
Oh! with what fury now Ororik burn'd!
  In fell revenge alone, his heart delighted—
Of guilt and innocence he scarce discern'd
  The difference, so his bosom was benighted:
And in the face of Heaven he swore, his hand
Should make a wilderness of Leinster's land.

XVII.

But further now before my tale proceeds,
  It seems a fit occasion to display
Before the man, or boy my work who reads—
  (For ladies long ere this, I fear, will lay
My book aside, for Arthur's noble deeds;
  For Marmion, Lalla Rookh, the minstrel's Lay—
Don Juan, or the Waverleys by scores:
Bright offspring of the Byrons, Scotts, or Moores.

XVIII

To please the ladies is my dear delight;
For I have had a sister and a mother—
I have a wife, and if I could but write
The bliss they beam on husband, son and brother,
Scarce Heaven itself could purer joys unite,
Life to embellish, or bestow another.
I *had* a daughter--darling of my love—
She is an angel in the realms above.

XIX.

No mortal on this earth then, better knows
The charms that women scatter o'er our lives;
Or more intensely feels the bliss that flows
From them, as sisters, mothers, daughters, wives.
But then I must admit, in verse or prose,
The dull and tedious seldom with them thrives:
They cannot bear a wearisome composer,
And from their very souls despise a proser.

XX.

The ladies then, I fear have flung aside
My book already, and I scarce can blame them—
It tells the story of a faithless bride,
And they may think the poet means to shame them.
Ah no! how many are the sex's pride!
They tell by thousands, and I here could name them;
I show one sinning woman for example:
What swarms of *men* on all their duties trample!

XXI.

But I was saying, man or boy who reads
My tale, should something of fair Erin know:
A map of all the country first he needs;
But that was not the same so long ago...
Of their great chiefs, should learn the lofty breeds;
Their laws, their customs, manners high and low:
How can I satisfy each prying elf;
Who know so little of all this myself?

XXII.

But what I do know I shall truly tell:
And to all future time, for truth bequeath:
Five kings did then within the island dwell;
Of Connaught, Leinster Munster, Ulster, Meath.
Kingdoms they were, which Grandgousier might well
Have taken in his time between his teeth:
To know Grandgousier if it ne'er befel you—
Consult old Rabelais, and he will tell you.

XXIII.

The lords of these same kingdoms, were called kings
And each in his dominions had some sway:
Not such indeed as from obedience springs,
Of subjects long accustom'd to obey—
The lords themselves could compass but small things,
As each by fighting, best could win his way:
The reader must not think those monarchs then,
Had armies of five hundred thousand men.

XXIV.

Between them often border wars arose,
  And each in turn encroach'd upon his neighbor;
So eager are mankind to fall to blows;
  So much, to rob, more ready than to labor;
Of justice savage man but little knows;
  His right is force, his title is his sabre;
And still, like Brennus of the Roman tale,
He flings his falchion in the balanc'd scale.

XXV.

Among those kings there arose from time to time,
  One braver or more skilful than the rest:
With brighter parts, and genius more sublime,
  Who bore among them all a loftier crest:
His power while in the vigor of his prime,
  O'er the whole island was at once impress'd:
And at the time precise of which I sing,
Roderick O'Connor was fair Erin's king,

XXVI

And then, the people were, as they are now,
  A careless, thoughtless, brave, kind hearted race:
With boiling bosom, and with dauntless brow,
  With shrewdest humor, and with laughing face:
Their women, purer than the virgin's vow,
  Blooming in beauty, and adorned with grace:
But some exceptions, I must own, were there,
As in all ages may be found elsewhere.

XXVII

Christians they had been from St. Patrick's day:
Their priests for learning had been long renown'd:
Though not accustomed Peter's pence to pay;
Nor homage to the pontiff triple crown'd.
Music they lov'd: they lov'd the minstrel's lay:
Their hearts were tun'd to harmony of sound:
As if from heaven's most hallow'd notes it stole,
The harp of Erin search'd the inmost soul.

XXVIII.

Ororik now sent round the fiery cross;
And call'd his liegemen to attend their lord;
Avenge his honor and redeem his loss.
They came in crowds, for Dermot was abhòrr'd:
To serve their prince they deem'd their lives as dross;
Each had two spears, a battle-axe and sword;
For Erin's sons, in that age, scorn did feel,
To case their limbs in panoply of steel.

XXIX.

And to the common monarch of the Isle
The prince of Breffny sent and claim'd his aid;
The messenger obtain'd the royal smile;
And a close alliance was between them made:
The object to extort from Dermot vile,
His beautious prize—his kingdom to invade:
Relieve his subjects from the tyrant's sway;
And hunt him, like a savage beast of prey.

XXX.

Anon, Ororik musters all his bands;
Of horse, and foot, battalion and platoon;
And mounts his steed, and issues his commands,
And from his castle sallies forth at noon.
Ere the next morning Fernes beleaguer'd stands;
Where Dermot's revels yet outwatch'd the moon.
Surpris'd, surrounded in the dead of night—
Defence was useless, his resort was flight.

XXXI.

Protected by the shades of night he fled;
And through Ororik's guards in safety past;
Asham'd, scarce knowing where to hide his head;
And scarcely clad to meet the morning blast.
He left the partner of his guilty bed—
Herself before her husband's knees she cast;
And to the saints with streaming tears appeal'd,
That force alone to Dermot made her yield.

XXXII.

For e'en ere Dermot was without the walls,
Ororik's eager host had forc'd their way,
In swarming crowds had fill'd the castle's halls;
And sought the chamber where the lady lay:
A din of noise confus'd her heart appals;
She springs from bed in terror and dismay.
And finds, (in wild disorder all her charms,)
Protection only in her husband's arms.

XXXIII.

Ororik now determin'd to retire ;
  But first gave orders closest search to make,
For Dermot, and the castle then to fire :
  And Fernes, from Dermot all retreat to take.
The convent only could escape his ire ;
  By Dermot founded, circled by a lake:
The rest to pillage and destruction given ;
Spar'd was the convent, heritage of Heaven.

XXXIV.

" And where is Agnes ?—where is Teague," he cries.
  Agnes and Teague fall prostrate at his feet ;
Imploring for their lives—he bids them rise,
  And to their lady give attendance meet.
The castle soon, a blazing ruin lies—
  Ororik's heart exults.—Revenge is sweet—
But oh ! must Fernes, must the whole city burn ;
For *one* man's crime ? has mercy no return ?

XXXV.

" It must,," exclaim'd the prince incens'd—" it shall ;
  Nor saint nor angel shall arrest my hand."
Fernes was defenceless, and the town was small—
  Albeit, metropolis of Leinster's land—
For its lord's vices destin'd now to fall,
  It kindled soon beneath the blazing brand :
In flames involv'd the wicked and the good ;
And ravens croak'd where Fernes before had stood.

XXXVI.

But oh! what mortal pencil e'er shall dare,
  Attempt to paint the horrors of that day?
What voice repeat the shrieks of wild despair,
  As wrapp'd in flames the cherish'd mansions lay?
How many orphans' fathers perish'd there!
  How many widows wail'd o'er lifeless clay;
Of slaughter'd sires and husbands dear, who fell,
In struggles vain the invader to repel!

XXXVII.

Ororik saw the blaze at first with joy;
  It was revenge, 't was perfidy chastis'd.
Such pleasures soon in generous bosoms cloy:
  At his own rage, he was at last surpris'd:
Alas! too late! 't was still the tale of Troy.
  When Heaven's avenging justice is despis'd--
Old Homer's moral ever will apply
Kings are the culprits,--and the people die.

XXXVIII.

Ororik now return'd; dismiss'd his bands;
  Forgot his wrongs and soon forgave his wife:
On Erin's annals it recorded stands,
  They led henceforth an exemplary life:
Of all the past the lady wash'd her hands;
  And shunn'd thereafter matrimonial strife:
They pass'd in peace the remnant of their lives—
He, a fond husband, she, the best of wives.

XXXIX.

Just so it happen'd, after Troy's sad fate,
  When with her husband, Menelaus, Helen
Return'd to Sparta's walls in royal state;
  And dropp'd the tripod which the ocean fell in;
And ages after, I forget the date,
  Fish'd up, was sent (the story as they tell in
Plutarch and Marmontel) all Greece around;
To find the wisest man, who ne'er was found.

XL.

But of the Irish lady I must own
  That I have heard another story told;
That she for some weeks was confined alone,
  And ever after found her husband cold;
Who sent her to her friends, where to atone
  For frailties past, she lavish'd showers of gold,
On holy church, of which the retribution,
Was to receive the prelate's absolution.

XLI.

In fresh pursuit of Dermot fifty men
  Had been despatch'd, but he their search eluded;
For rufuge fled to forest, wild, or glen;
  Or climb'd an oak, as once, Charles Stuart, you did;
Or lurk'd conceal'd, in cavern or in den,
  By hunger pinch'd, of raiment near denuded.
And after suffering more than ever man did,
Took ship at Dublin, and at Bristol landed.

XLII.

And here he found among the sons of trade
Jews, tender hearted souls, who money lent,
And freely furnished charitable aid,
On good security, at cent per cent ;
And banish'd kings, and ruin'd spendthrifts made
Their special care, in kind compassion meant—
And for a mortgage of his whole domain,
With means supplied him to reach Aquitaine.

XLIII.

For there the royal court of Albion's king,
Henry Plantagenet, was held in state ;
He, who by virtue of Pope Adrian's ring
Became the arbiter of Erin's fate.
Though at his heart far less inclin'd to cling
To crosier titles at the present date—
To him, the grantor of another's throne,
He found, might to another grant his own.

XLIV.

For sturdy Becket, Canterbury's saint,
Had turn'd the realm of Albion upside down :
Because, regardless of his just complaint,
And in defiance of the triple crown ;
Henry had dar'd the primate's rights to taint ;
And cast his mitre's bold pretentions down :
And at some pageant (who can give it credence ?)
To York's archbishop had assign'd precedence.

XLV.

Oh! love of place! is there in earth's wide span,
  To sway the human heart, a fiercer passion;
Saint Becket was a meek and humble man;
  To prayer devoted as was then the fashion—
And whensoever into sin he ran,
  Prepar'd himself smartly to lay the lash on.
But sooner than resign one inch of place,
In ruin would have sunk the human race.

XLVI.

And thus was Henry with the Pope engag'd,
  In quarrels, at that time no joking thing:
His sons against him war rebellious wag'd;
  And he was ill at ease with France's King;
With Becket he became so much enrag'd
  Soon after!—but of that I shall not sing—
It was not then his time—(I hate digression,)
Of Ireland for himself to take possession.

XLVII.

But Dermot was a suitor at his court;
  And offer'd homage to him as his lord;
Made of his own expulsion a report;
  And to his kingdom pray'd to be restor'd—
He own'd that female conquest was his forte;
  Confess'd that Breffny's wife he had a lor'd:
This was mere gallantry in Henry's eyes;
Himself a mint of lechery and lies.

XLVIII.

Himself a traitor to the marriage bed;
And punish'd bitterly as never fails;
Of his fair Rosamond you all have read;
And of his household jars may read the tales:
His wife, his sons conspir'd against his head;
And brought him to the grave, if truth avails:
The direst ills the human heart can know,
From wedlock's broken bonds, forever flow.

XLIX.

To Dermot's offers, Henry gave assent;
And of his homage liege receiv'd the vow:
To give him aid declar'd his full intent;
Though not prepar'd for expedition now.
But under the great seal an instrument
Despatch'd, his loving subjects to allow,
In Dermot's cause fair Erin to invade;
While his own preparations should be made.

L.

Thus furnish'd, Dermot back to Bristol hies,
There, and in Wales his letters patent shews:
And levies troops to share the tempting prize;
And moves again the tender hearted Jews;
Obtains of men and moneys large supplies;
And calls on all the spirits bold, who choose
Of noble deeds to kindle at the flame,
To join his standard for the fields of fame.

LI.

Nor was the summons of the chieftain vain:
  For bold adventurers were not wanting there;
And near the borders of the Welsh domain
  Dwelt Richard Strongbow of the house of Clare:
A man who of retainers kept a train,
  Addicted more to pillage than to prayer:
Himself of morals reprobate and base;
And at the monarch's court in deep disgrace.

LII.

And far in Wales, on lofty Snowden's side:
  And in a fastness of Plinlimmon fam'd;
Two base born sons of Nesta did reside;
  Fitz-Stephen one, and one Fitz-Gerald nam'd:
Men who the laws of God and man defied;
  Of fortunes ruin'd, of lives unreclaim'd—
With troops of followers like themselves, renown'd:
What fitter men for Dermot could be found?

LIII.

Fitz-Stephen and his brother both by chance
  Were then at Bristol, and with Dermot met;
A few days after his return from France,
  And while contracting with the Jews his debt.
Need was there, they agreed, that in advance,
  Dermot on Erin's shore his foot should set.
And there, in secret lurking, first alone;
To clear his way, raise forces of his own.

LIV.

And winter thus would pass, and when the spring
Return'd, the sons of Nesta both agreed,
A troop of valiant archers each to bring,
To join the standard and for Dermot bleed:
Provided, when he should again be king
Of praise and booty they should share the meed.
Of conquer'd lands a portion fair should hold,
And on the list of nobles stand enroll'd.

LV.

But upon terms thus cheap, the aid of Clare
Could not be purchas'd--he had higher aims:
A band more numerous to the field could bear;
And spread o'er Erin more destructive flames.
He claim'd the hand of Dermot's daughter fair:
Eva, for beauty, among Erin's dames
By none surpass'd, few equall'd, in renown:
The future heiress too of Dermot's crown.

LVI.

And Dermot promis'd him fair Eva's hand;
And thus his country and his daughter sold—
Oh! who can read the record of that land,
And mark her miseries with bosom cold?
If it must boil to see before us stand,
A wretch who barters liberty for gold;
To see one, with what anguish must it swell,
At once himself, his child, his country sell.

LVII.

Among the critics it has been of yore,
A question whether, when he forms his plan,
An epic poet must, to say no more,
Take for his hero a right honest man.
But I for my part hold the rule a bore;
'T were well to make him honest if you can;
Into another question it must fall;
Where such a hero can be found at-all.

LVIII.

"Heroes are much the same (so Pope avers,)
From Macedonia's madman to the Swede."
But this again, another question stirs;
If after ages have improv'd the breed!
And to my memory only one occurs
Adapted to disturb the poet's creed.
Will any mortal ask—who is that one?
Name him! Ay! hold a taper to the Sun!

LIX.

'T is said, the exception only proves the rule—
All other heroes from the days of Pope,
Compounds have been of madman, knave and fool,
And thus may be defin'd, without a trope.
All servile followers of the self same school:
Who hang themselves, whenever they have rope.
Till time shall end, their merits you may scan;
Among them ere you find one honest man.

LX.

So far then from improvement in the breed,
  The scale has fallen since the poet's days—
For Charles of Sweden, raving mad indeed,
  Deserves at least, of honesty the praise.
Taught Quintus Curtius, when a boy, to read,
  It fir'd his brain, and madden'd all his days.
Till his fate led him to the "barren strand,
The petty fortress, and the dubious hand."

LXI.

You then who purpose to invoke the Muse,
  And in the cause of virtue point the pen;
Need take no thought, your subjects when you choose
  To look for heroes among honest men:
Stout hearts, fierce passions, lusts to shame the stews,
  And mercy, fitted for the tiger's den;
These are your heroes of the last disclosure;
Who blood and slaughter see with due composure.

LXII.

But e'en from these, the moral maxim draw—
  Strip off their laurels and expose their lives:
Bound by no tie of liberty or law,
  False to their country—traitors to their wives.
Strip to the skin, and hold them not in awe—
  Bare to the bone—with lancets and with knives:
And teach the world, from Nimrod down to Nero,
What sort of skeleton can make a hero.

LXIII.

And this, my countrymen, is my design,
In calling Dermot from the shades below :
And Albion's Henry of the Norman line,
Albeit they liv'd six hundred years ago.
The tale I tell is no device of mine :
Plain, simple, bare historic truth I show :
Of Erin's wrongs, the origin I trace—
How and by whom the conquest first took place.

LXIV.

It has been said that Lucan's lofty lay,
Is nothing more than a gazette in rhyme :
And of my poem you the same may say—
But, read the chronicles of olden time—
And with injustice charge not me, I pray ;
If I name persons deeply sunk in crime :
For Dermot, Henry, Nesta's sons, and Clare,
I only bring before you as they were.

LXV.

No honest man among them you shall find ;
And I could grieve for them with all my heart.
But then in such a scheme, to speak my mind,
No honest man would ever take a part.
Six hundred years since then have gone behind ;
Still Erin bleeds, beneath Britannia's dart :
Still for the moralist the task remains,
To mark by whom and how were forg'd her chains.

LXVI.

Six hundred years! oppression has her date—
  Expect not I shall tell that tale of woe—
In tears, in blood, I cannot write her fate:
  And Erin's hand is rais'd to strike the blow.
Her harp to Freedom strung, she stands sedate:
  No more a slave, her tyrants soon shall know.
Soon shall she stand, (earth! heaven! unite in cheers;)
An independent State amidst her peers.

DERMOT MAC MORROGH.

CANTO III.

THE RESTORATION.

I.

WHEN Dermot's treaties with his brave allies
  And with his thrifty Jews were sign'd and seal'd :
His next concern was, measures to devise,
  To reach his realm, beneath disguise's shield.
The reader, I need not again apprise,
  Of what a former canto has reveal'd :
That Dermot, to lay up in heaven a store,
A convent founded, some short time before.

II.

"Lay up in heaven your store," was Christ's command;
  "Which neither moth shall e'er corrupt, nor rust."
But some there were, who then did understand,
  That to build convents was to raise a trust :
That heaven was bound for every inch of land,
  Granted, to make remuneration just—
And Dermot claim'd, for every farthing lent,
Just like the Jews at Bristol, cent per cent.

III.

He built a convent for Augustin friars;
  Call'd from the tincture of their garments, "black"—
Whoso, the history of that age inquires,
  To meet these holy monks, shall not be slack—
And whosoever, at this day desires
  Not far from Ludgate Hill to call a hack;
Shall see the only remnant of their names,
In an old bridge that crosses o'er the Thames.

IV.

In Dermot's time they were a potent order;
  Whose vows of poverty, large wealth repaid:
Whose vows of chastity, cost much disorder:
  And of obedience, princes of them made.
O'er every hill and valley, plain and border
  Of Christendom they drove their gainful trade:
And soon receiv'd from Innocent the Third
Powers to crush heresies, and preach the word.

V.

And, undiscover'd now his home to reach,
  Dermot, in furtherance of his purpose foul,
Assumes the monkish garb as if to preach;
  The shaven crown, beard, rosary and cowl.
Then ships from Bristol, lands on Erin's beach:
  Near Wexford, there to loiter and to prowl:
And thence, by nightly stolen steps returns,
To his own monkish mansion-house at Fernes.

VI.

Here, lingering through the winter in disguise,
He lurk'd, the ghostly brotherhood among:
Enlisted forces for his enterprise,
And matins with the friars, and vespers sung.
Sent them throughout the region round, as spies,
To preach, until the people's hearts were stung:
That Dermot though expell'd, was Leinster's king,
And from abroad o'erwhelming force would bring.

VII.

But, that he could not thus conceal'd remain,
Through the long winter months may be surmis'd.
And Roderick, lord of Erin's whole domain,
Of his concealment shortly was appris'd.
The convent walls themselves, asylum vain,
Would prove to Dermot as he was advis'd—
So, gathering all the vassals that he could,
Trembling, he fled for shelter to the wood.

VIII.

By Erin's king and Breffny's prince pursued,
Against them twice he dar'd maintain the fight;
But soon perceiving he must be subdued,
A wily stratagem preferr'd to flight—
Ambrose, a monk, he sent with craft endued;
To represent with tears his piteous plight:
To promise humble homage in his name,
And even Linster's lordship to disclaim.

IX.

Ten cantreds (1) only for himself he crav'd,
Of Erin's king in fealty to hold ;
And all the remnant of his princedom waiv'd,
And proffer'd hostages and promise'd gold.
And of Ororik, as he would be sav'd,
Implor'd forgiveness for offences old :
Stripp'd as he was of property and right ;
Sure he no longer umbrage could excite.

X.

And Roderick listen'd to the smooth-tongued friar ;
And Dermot's vows and hostages receiv'd,
Ororik quench'd his old resentment's fire,
From instant ruin Dermot was reliev'd :
The fraud succeeded to his heart's desire :
But he no sooner found himself retriev'd,
Than all his promises dissolved in air ;
The hostages were left their fate to bear.

XI.

For soon, too soon, in Erin's evil hour,
Fitz-Stephen landed on her hapless strand :
He came the herald of Britannia's power,
He came to conquer and subdue the land.
Alas ! was Erin's genius doom'd to cower,
Before the fortunes of that paltry band ?
Three hundred archers, coats of mail three score,
And thirty knights came with him, AND NO MORE !

XII.

Fitz-Stephen landed at the Bay of Bann,
And straight a messenger to Dermot sent;
Recurring to their joint concerted plan,
And his own hopes to compass that event.
And now this faithless, this perfidious man,
The air with shouts of joyous transport rent:
And call'd his vassals up to share the spoil:
And join the invader of his native soil.

XIII.

Assembled at the beach of Bann they met;
And marching thence in well combin'd array,
Towards Wexford's town their faces first they set;
Of Albion's conquest the first destined prey:
And there you find the town and harbor yet,
At twelve miles' distance standing from the bay.
First fruit of Erin's servitude accurst:
And now to hail her freedom too the first.

XIV.

Assail'd thus suddenly and unprepar'd,
At once by robbery and treason's force;
That Wexford's peaceful citizens were scar'd,
And stunn'd with terror you may judge of course:
And yet, no bloodless prize the victor shar'd,
Her bravest blood was Wexford's sole resource.
The foe's first onset met repulsion just,
And twenty bold assailants bit the dust.

XV.

But soon Fitz-Stephen to the charge return'd,
His horsemen's armor glitter'd from afar,
His archers with redoubled ardor burn'd;
The coat of mail reflects a dazzling star.
Their stipend, traitrous emissaries earn'd,
And magnified the terrors of the war.
While holy men of God in Dermot's pay,
Abus'd the name of Heaven, for peace to pray.

XVI.

And so they sent at last a deputation,
With two right reverend bishops at its head;
And sign'd with Dermot a capitulation,
And vow'd new homage to their sovereign, dread:
While he in turn, by counter-stipulation
To Nesta's sons transferr'd them in his stead:
And Wexford thus, with all the region round:
Of Albion's vassals now became the ground.

XVII.

Unhallow'd compact! Covenant impure!
Is there in human form a soul so base?
Or shall there be, while earth and heaven endure,
A fouler stain of unredeem'd disgrace?
Oh! let no lapse of ages e'er obscure,
No distance veil, of infamy the trace!
Record, ye angles, on the rolls of shame;
Record in deathless darkness, Dermot's name.

XVIII.

For this, of Erin's conquest, was the pledge,
  This, to the distant tyrant, footing gave.
This, of her primal servitude, the wedge,
  The spade, portentous of her freedom's grave.
Rivers of Erin, trim with wo your sedge!
  Mountains, your hoary heads in sadness wave!
Plains, forests, wilds, in mournful vestments stand!
Henceforth a *foreign* master rules the land.

XIX.

But Dermot's bosom, kindling with success,
  To other aim and purpose now was fir'd:
His fell ambition now to nothing less
  Than of all Erin to be king aspir'd
His savage passion others to oppress,
  A more extensive theatre desir'd—
To crush his king! Ororik to destroy!
The very vision swell'd his soul with joy.

XX.

Designs thus bold must be matur'd by time;
  And Dermot's forces needed some repose—
His brightening prospects, darken'd more his crime;
  All crime successful, more gigantic grows.
To make the purpose of Fitz-Stephen chime
  With his own projects; now he did propose;
And courteously engag'd at Fernes, his friend
The festal days of Whitsuntide to spend.

XXI.

And thither with their forces they repair,
  And yield their hours to jollity and mirth—
The night's carousal, and the morning's prayer
  Mingling with hopes of heaven the joys of earth.
While Dermot's secret toilsome thoughts prepare
  To bring his distant deep designs to birth ;
But dare not to Fitz-Stephen yet unroll
The hidden purpose of his secret soul.

XXII.

There was between him and a neighboring chief
  Of Ossory, a feud of ancient date :
A son of Dermot slain had caus'd him grief ;
  And now he purpos'd to avenge his fate.
Fitz-Stephen said he came to bring relief,
  And Dermot's foes wherever found, to mate :
He and his bands were ready to proceed ;
And for him fight, wherever he should lead.

XXIII.

And forth they went, and with no sparing hand
  O'er Ossory's harvests fire and ruin spread:
The prince of Ossory rais'd a faithful band;
  Who made against the mingled legions, head.
With various fortune, war's destructive brand
  Was brandish'd—blood in blended torrents shed :
Till Britain's hireling bands at length prevail'd
And Ossory's churls before their victors quail'd.

XXIV.

Three hundred heads of slaughter'd foes were brought,
To Dermot, who beheld them with delight;
And dar'd from lips with foul pollution fraught,
To thank the God of mercy for that sight.
One ghastly face, between his teeth he caught,
With foaming rage to mangle and to bite.
To such extremes can human frenzy go,
To glut revenge upon a fallen foe.

XXV.

Yet were the men of Ossory not subdued:
Led by their prince the invaders they repell'd,
They fought, by turns assailants and pursued;
One day victorious and another quell'd:
Till weary of the warfare that ensued,
A solemn treaty they with Dermot held.
As their liege lord acknowledging his sway.
And took his pledge to send his troops away.

XXVI.

But what were treaties, what to him was shame?
Fitzgerald now had join'd him with his band;
Against them Roderick and Ororik came,
To drive the foreign bandit from the land.
Of these dire hunters Ireland was the game:
Not Dermot's self their force could now withstand;
And Erin's monarch struggled all in vain,
From their firm grasp to rescue his domain.

XXVII.

In fancied hope, their councils to divide
He sends a messenger to each apart;
Assails the British chieftains by their pride;
Probes the dark avenues of Dermot's heart—
Reminds the Britons of the stolen bride;
The perjur'd promises, the treacherous art:
The ruthless murders of their vile compeer;
And all the crimes that blacken'd his career.

XXVIII.

"Mine," said O'Conner, "is the lawful sway,
Of all the shores, Hibernia's ocean laves—
My sceptre, all her princely chiefs obey;
My power the lord alone of Leinster braves:
No wrong to Erin's charge can Britain lay:
Sever'd by ocean's all surrounding waves.
Can high-soul'd British knights endure the shame
Of league avow'd with Dermot's blasted fame?

XXIX.

"Not mine the purpose, with intrepid knights,
To threats of peril, or their fears appeal—
My own authority; my country's rights;
Are sureyl motives they themselves must feel.
My numerous host to confidence invites;
And absent thousands yet may prove their zeal:
But blood and carnage are not my desire;
I only wish the Britons to retire.

XXX.

"They and their chieftains shall in safety pass:
To this I freely pledge my royal word.
With confirmation of the holy mass:
Such my repugnance is to draw the sword.
Nor shall conveyance fail for every class
Of warriors—neither shall they be demurr'd—
Nor even call'd for passage home to pay:
Myself the costs and charges will defray."

XXXI.

The sons of Nesta, with expressive smile,
Heard Roderick's messenger his task perform:
And gave him charge in most respectful style,
Their answer to return in courtly form.
"Their purpose was not, from the verdant isle
To ship, but there to meet the coming storm:
To reinstate Lord Dermot on his throne,
Maintain his rights, and vindicate their own.

XXXII.

"They saw with pleasure and sincere applause,
King Roderick's reverence for the nuptial tie;
And mark'd his own observance of those laws;
In his own progeny of doubtful die—
But it was no concern of theirs, to pause,
Into the pastimes of the great to pry.
If sometimes, ladies had been found to roam,
It might be, they had met neglect at home.

XXXIII.

"Indeed, to speak their sentiments sincere,—
They know not why, *to them*, King Roderick sent—
If to announce he had commenc'd a seer;
It could not be a prophet that he meant—
If to command as king, it should appear;
Their king he was not—they must still dissent;
If finally, he threaten'd as a foe—
With their defiance let his envoy go."

XXXIV.

Rejected thus with contumelious scorn—
To Dermot's self the envoy next applied.
On Erin's land reminds him he was born—
The land where his forefathers liv'd and died,
His native country wretched and forlorn,
Beheld him now against herself allied.
And now by Roderick's warning voice implores
To shake the foreign robber from her shores.

XXXV.

Of past dissensions he would say no more:
King Roderick would forget them and forgive—
Their strife the common mother must deplore;
She wish'd her sons in harmony to live:
To peace would Dermot open wide the door
Dismission to his Britons let him give—
And to his kingdom instantly restor'd;
Reign henceforth Leinster's undisputed lord.

XXXVI.

To Roderick's sovereign rule, he must submit ;
   And send his British hireling troops away :
A patriot sure must deem it far more fit,
   To bear a native lord, than foreign sway.
His Britons, whate'er he might think of it ;
   Would turn to masters at no distant day—
And Dermot's name in after times would stand,
Stamp'd to all ages with the traitor's brand.

XXXVII.

Let him then listen to his country's call ;
   And bid forthwith his foreign files depart :
Should their resentment on him chance to fall,
   King Roderick was at hand to make them smart.
Expel them, or exterminate them all ;
   And ease the terrors of each honest heart :
While Dermot's name should reap, redeem'd to fame,
A patriot's glory for a traitor's shame.

XXXVIII.

But if this warning voice he should despise ;
   And lean on foreign ruffians for support;
One common ruin him and his allies
   Would overtake ; and their career be short.
For every heart which freedom's worth could prize,
   Would rally round King Roderick and his court :
And bear, with him, till their expiring breath,
The freeman's banner—liberty or death.

XXXIX.

But Dermot's callous soul, to virtue blind,
  The message flouted and the envoy spurn'd;
Gave flat refusal but no cause assign'd;
  And Roderick's envoy to his camp return'd.
And now, all hope of peace or truce resign'd,
  Fierce for the battle either army burn'd.
And every breast dejected or elate,
With fear and hope awaited Erin's fate.

XL.

But ere the hosts were marshall'd for the fight,
  Each adverse chieftain his own band address'd—
And urg'd, their martial ardor to excite,
  Whate'er could fire, and animate the breast.
"Friends!" said O'Conner, "we contend for right—
  For every blessing by mankind possessed;
Alike defend the cottage and the throne—
The prize for us at stake is all our own.

XLI.

Not for *their* own, yon motley hordes contend;
  By British bastards and by Dermot led;
Dermot, the vile traducer of his friend;
  And foul disturber of the nuptial bed:
Wont all the bonds of property to rend;
  And draw the avenging bolt upon his head:
Now, not content himself to hurl the brand,
Brings foreign robbers to consume the land.

XLII.

" Their wives—their children! what is there in life,
Can be more dear to human kind, than these?
But each of you must here defend his wife:
Defend the child he dandles on his knees:
These are for you the victims of the strife,
Should you . . . . . I feel the blood within me freeze. . .
Your choice is freedom, honorable graves,
Or to behold your wives and children slaves.

XLIII.

Slaves to rude ruffians from a foreign shore;
To cringe, and fawn, and bend the servile knee:
Yet hold, to rive the tortur'd bosom more;
The bitter memory that they once were free—
March then, the conflict sharp will soon be o'er;
March! to the foe then! . . Sooner die than flee—
And trust (his finger pointed to the sky)
" Trust Him—the ruler of the worlds on high."

XLIV.

"March!" echoed as he spoke, each Irish heart—
And brandish'd high the battle-ax in air,
While Dermot and Fitz Stephen on their part,
Each his own troop harangued with equal care—
Dermot, the soldiers' sympathy, with art,
To raise, the fame of Roderick did not spare:
Not against Erin he declar'd he came;
But his own right, his kingdom to reclaim.

XLV.

"By Roderick and by Breffny's prince expell'd;
With brave allies behold your lord come back—
King Roderick always in fair speech excell'd:
His words are soothing, as his *heart is black;*
And, never satisfied with what he held,
In blood and slaughter you shall mark his track.
His purpose is to govern like a god;
And rule all Erin with an iron rod."

XLVI.

Fitz Stephen other motives to his bands
Urges—"We came an injur'd prince to aid.
That prince by large and noble grants of lands
Our faithful service promptly has repaid:
Of ancient record, British valor stands:
Her dictates now again must be obey'd:
Neglected, slighted, in our native land:
Wealth, fame, and honors we may here command."

XLVII.

And now while deeds of death each bosom fire,
And expectation pants to be releas'd—
While war's fierce furies every heart inspire;
Impatient, waiting for the vulture's feast;
In Dermot and Fitz Stephen's camp, a friar
Propos'd to meet with Roderick's shiving priest:
And in the name of holy church desir'd
A last attempt for peace as she requir'd.

XLVIII.

And Roderick yielded to religion's claim;
  And to the proffer'd meeting gave consent:
Half way between the camps the churchmen came;
  And form'd a compact which might all content.
A skilful compromise compos'd its frame.
  Concession from each side was its intent—
And if in Dermot's faith could have been trust,
The league had lasting been, for it was just.

XLIX.

The lawful power of Roderick, Dermot own'd;
  As reaching o'er all Erin's hills and dales.
And by a secret tie himself he bound,
  To send his Welsh confederates back to Wales:
And swore that never more on Irish ground
  To tread, should troops auxiliar spread their sails.
And now suspicion's lightest shades to shun:
He gave for hostage his most favor'd son.

L.

And Connaught's monarch on his part engag'd,
  Forth from the field his forces to withdraw;
That war no more on Dermot should be wag'd,
  And Leinster might again receive his law.
Yet more, to quench the rancor which had rag'd,
  And closest ties of amity to draw,
O'Conner pledg'd his daughter in alliance
With Dermot's son, the hostage, to affiance.

LI.

The league was struck! and Erin was undone!
  Uncrush'd the foreign hydra's head remain'd:
The occasion lost, again was never won;
  And Dermot's perfidy was unrestrain'd:
To Roderick's mercy he resign'd his son;
  His oath, his treaty to regard disdain'd;
The hapless hostage, for a promis'd bride,
The victim of his father's falsehood died.

LII.

The British brothers saw the parley held;
  And soon had notice of the treaty made;
The secret compact was from them withheld;
  But soon by Dermot, with the rest betray'd.
Dermot had promis'd they should be expell'd—
  What if in time, he ceas'd to need their aid?—
For who a traitor's favors can regard?
Distrust and hatred are their just reward.

LIII.

Fitz Stephen mark'd with cool observant eye,
  The properties of Dermot's heart and mind:
And straight resolv'd to trust his dear ally;
  So far as just occasion he should find.
He could not rate his truth to promise high,
  And thought for other means his faith to bind:
But thought of none so likely to endure
As granite wall to make his bargain sure.

LIV.

But still to treat with courtesy his friend,
He made the men of Wexford his pretence:
The place from their defection to defend,
He urg'd, on Dermot not to give offence?
Dermot, he knew, could not on them depend;
And with his aid, a short time, could dispense:
And thus obtain'd from Dermot's royal court
His free permission to erect a fort.

LV.

Of Erin's cities Dublin is the prime
Borne on the wave and facing Albion's coast:
For ages growing with the lapse of time,
Now of the verdant Isle the pride and boast—
Founded by pirates from the northern clime,
And in that age by them frequented most;
Retaining, though she now no more retains,
Remnants of conquests by the valiant Danes.

LVI.

Within the bounds of Dermot's realm she fell:
Bnt never had been subject to his sway:
Against his father she had dar'd rebel,
And driven by force his officers away.
Himself, attempting her revolt to quell
Had fall'n by murder's hand in fierce affray:
And then, as if his son's revenge to brave;
Had with a dog been buried in one grave.

LVII.

But now, by Roderick's forces check'd no more,
Dermot indulg'd his passion, long suppress'd:
Resolv'd on Dublin his whole host to pour,
And glut the vengeance boiling in his breast.
He storm'd the city, fill'd her streets with gore;
And slaughter'd thousands nor had spar'd the rest—
But Nesta's son for respite interceded,
And for their pardons, helpless wretches! pleaded.

LVIII.

This cruel butchery throughout the land
The people struck with horror and dismay:
No more protected by their monarch's brand;
They flew for refuge to the tyrant's sway—
Flock'd to his bloody standard; kiss'd his hand;
Implor'd his pardon; promis'd to obey:
Again acknowledg'd him their lawful lord;
And Dermot to his kingdom was restor'd.

NOTE (1) STANZA IX.

A cantred (as Giraldus saith) is a word compounded of the British and of the Irish tongues, and containeth so much ground as wherein are one hundred villages, which in England is termed a *hundred*.
Hooker's Translation of Giraldus, Ch. 2 p. 4.

DERMOT MAC MORROGH.

CANTO IV.

THE CONQUEST.

I.

AMBITION (saith a sage who far had kenn'd,
Into the wily windings of the heart,)
Ambition, when she seeks a certain end,
Deceives herself with hypocritic art:
That end obtain'd, her purposes to bend
Becomes a means, another end to start.
Such, of the plumeless biped is the fashion:
Ambition is a never ending passion.

II.

Ambition, therefore, virtue is, or vice;
Ting'd by the object of the man's pursuit;
A jewel, richer than the ruby's price;
A Bohon Uphas, bearing deadly fruit.
Ethereal fire, impenetrable ice:
The good supreme; of every ill the root:
A guardian angel, leading to the skies—
A demon, with the worm that never dies.

III.

Teach not your children then to shun ambition;
  Nor quench the flame that must forever burn;
But in the days of infancy, their vision
  To deeds of virtue and of glory turn:
Of man, their mortal brother, the condition
  To mend, improve, and elevate to learn:
Then, all the means they ever shall employ,
Will point to endless bliss, and boundless joy.

IV.

Not such the lesson Dermot had been taught:
  Not such at least the lesson he had learn'd:
With all ambition's fires his bosom fraught,
  For deeds of ruin and destruction burn'd—
His kingdom to recover he had fought:
  His British hirelings their reward had earn'd.
They had no motive longer to remain—
He none, their service longer to retain.

V.

But Leinster now no longer bounds his aim;
  He burns o'er all the verdant isle to reign;
The latent spark has kindled to a flame;
  And now he dares his purpose to explain;
Trumps up some worthless, old, forgotten claim:
  His vain pretence, with title to sustain:
Which Nesta's sons, impartially severe;
Pronounc'd at once indisputably clear.

VI.

And now he calls on them for their assistance;
 And paints the fruitfulness of Connaught's plains:
Assures them Roderick can make no resistance;
 And parcels out between them his domains;
But they, more prudent, counsel him, from distance,
 To summon Strongbow with his steel-clad swains.
And thus to bring a force upon the field,
Before which Roderick could not choose but yield.

VII.

But Dermot's bosom with impatience boils;
 And grudges sore the time it needs must take,
To summon Strongbow to partake the spoils:
 He strives in vain their firm resolves to shake.
They both had wives upon their native soils.
 Yet he to each proposes for a stake,
That very daughter, gentle soul'd and fair;
Whom he before, by treaty, sold to Clare.

VIII.

But Nesta's sons were not to be controll'd;
 And winter now invited to repose:
They flatter'd Dermot, own'd his project bold:
 But chance was fickle; they had watchful foes.
The force of Strongbow would give firmer hold:
 Connaught must fall, nor could withstand his blows:
And thus they urg'd, until at length the king
Deferr'd his purpos'd conquest till the spring.

IX.

And Dermot sent a messenger to Clare;
With letters urging him to come with speed—
Surprise avowing not to see him there,
As by the bond between them was agreed—
" The seasons pass,"—he said—" The birds of air,
The stork, the swallow, faithful to their breed,
Flock'd to our shores, and have again departed—
Earl Strongbow sure is equally true hearted.

X.

" But spring and autumn have by turns prevail'd;
Winter and summer held their fated course—
Yet I no signal of my friend have hail'd;
No aid experienc'd from his promis'd force—
My realm of Leinster, with my warriors mail'd,
I conquer'd—trac'd rebellion to her source.
And Nesta's sons, with princely fiefs invested,
My faith and fervent gratitude attested.

VI.

" My adverse fortunes they have nobly shar'd,
And came, redeemers from my sharp distress;
Nor blood nor fortune to relieve me spar'd;
And justly claim to share in my success:—
And now, a wider enterprise prepar'd,
If Strongbow, for his promis'd aid I press,
'Tis but REWARD I set before his eyes;
And not to share the peril, but the prize.

XII.

" My claim o'er all the verdant isle extends,
  Roderick O'Conner has usurp'd my right—
My title has been shown to faithful friends;
  Its justice is undoubted in their sight;
Connaught has fertile fields to make amends
  For all, my chiefs may suffer in the fight—
Come with thy archers—bend the fateful bow;
And lay the lofty pride of Roderick low.

XIII.

" The cause itself is more thy own than mine;
  The right recover'd can I long retain?
By sure transmission through the royal line,
  By nature's course it must with thee remain.
And here a blooming maid, with eyes divine
  Awaits thy coming, shall she wait in vain?
Come, Strongbow, come, my darling Eva's charms,
Shall hide their blushing beauties in thy arms."

XIV.

The love, the pride, the avarice of Clare,
  Were mov'd, by this epistle, with address:
His ruin'd fortunes stung him to despair:
  His king's displeasure scarcely stung him less;
By him unlicens'd he could never dare
  Expose his followers to the same distress:
He thought it best, the worst at once to meet:
And went and flung himself at Henry's feet.

XV.

Deplor'd the darkness of his favor lost:
  Implor'd the radiance of returning light:
Swore he had never by intention cross'd
  His will one instant, or defied his might:
Crav'd, though with hope and fear alternate toss'd,
  Permission to embark for Dermot's right:
And vow'd, that all the achievements of his sword,
Should only swell the trophies of his lord.

XVI.

The jealous tyrant, spurn'd his vassal base;
  And from his presence order'd him away:
But Clare accustom'd to endure disgrace,
  Abandon'd not, for one repulse his prey;
He sought again to meet the monarch's face—
  Sooth'd by submission, Henry's wrath gave way:
Some doubtful word he spoke, with gracious look,
Which Strongbow for his royal licence took.

XVII.

In two divisions he array'd his troops;
  And forward sent the first to land in May:
Harvey Mountmorres led this early group;
  A soul more ruthless never bred a fray,
With names to make the head of Mercy droop,
  And strike the heart of Pity with dismay,
Raymond le Gross, to Nesta's sons akin—
And Milo, high De Cogan—man of sin.

XVIII.

Near Waterford they landed, just below—
  And rais'd a trench around them for defence:
Portending to the sons of Erin wo:
  Nor could they now allege the old pretence;
Or shield the dark premeditated blow,
  With Dermot's rights--the scorn of common sense:
Invasion now—could have nought else in view,
Than Erin's Isle to plunder and subdue.

XIX.

And Waterford resounds with dire alarms;
  And panic terrors and confusion reign:
And concertless, her people fly to arms,
  And struggle for defence—alas! in vain—
Rush to the foe, in wild, unbounded swarms;
  Shock'd with repulse, retreat; advance again:
With valor cool the Britons meet the fire,
Yield to the clash, and to their Fort retire.

XX.

Ray d alrea y from the region round
  Had sent a party to provide subsistence,
Who gathering all the cattle to be found,
  Had driv'n them to the fortress, from far distance:
And now, disputing every inch of ground,
  The Britons from the bullocks drew assistance:
They drove the furious herds upon the foe;
As trampling, bellowing, goring, on they go.

XXI.

Reader, hast thou a Plutarch, near at hand?
Look to the life of Pyrrhus, thou shalt see,
That once, the valiant Romans, by a band
Of trampling elephants were made to flee.
And Flours says they never could withstand
Those animals till after battles three:
The first they lost; the second was drawn game;
The third they won, and after, kept them tame.

XXII.

The reader shall do well too, who perpends,
How this reverse of things was brought about;
And how the Roman soldier made amends
For his past cowardice, and grew more stout:
One, bolder than the rest, to gain his ends,
By a bold push, cut off the monster's snout--
And thus discover'd that the way to still them,
Was, as with other noxious beasts—to kill them.

XXIII.

But then the men of Waterford had not
Wit, this sublime discovery to make:
Yet, on their memory this should shed no blot;
The bullock phalanx, was too strong to break:
Of Romans and of Irishmen the lot
How much alike the reader here will take--
In parallel exact their story pulls;
With Roman elephants, and Irish bulls.

XXIV.

The British archers with the deadly dart,
  Pursue the scatter'd wretches as they flee:
And speed the shaft to many an Irish heart;
  And hundreds drive to perish in the sea.
Nor mercy to their captive foes impart,
  Though wealthy burghers, of the first degree.
The bloody Raymond would have spar'd their lives,
His fiercer chief made widows of their wives.

XXV.

Their only crime had been their native land
  From hordes of foreign robbers to defend,
And soon Earl Strongbow and his second band,
  On hapless Erin's fated shores descend—
And scarcely have they reach'd the destin'd strand,
  Before their march to Waterford they bend:
Take it by storm and slay without compassion
Man, woman, child, in high heroic fashion.

XXVI.

And sated carnage stays her hand at last;
  And shouts of victory float upon the gale;
And up to heaven ascends the mingled blast,
  The soldier's triumph, and the widow's wail:
And now to bind in ties of union fast;
  Ties which endure, when faith and honor fail;
Dermot comes forth, with royal pomp and pride;
And brings to Strongbow his intended bride.

XXVII.

Among the whimsies of the human brain,
A king there was, but I forgot his name:
Who once conceiv'd an ardent wish to gain
Of science mathematical the fame:
But, willing to dispense with all the pain
Of wasting years upon the taper's flame;
Sent for a grave professor of the art;
To learn the mathematics, all by heart.

XXVIII.

The Newton of the time bestow'd applause—
Upon the resolution of his pupil:
But brought his studies to a sudden pause—
By gentle intimation of a scruple;
And asking what he knew of number's laws
Already?—"Nothing."—Then he gave a blue pill,
By saying—"Please your majesty—I see
You first must learn the golden rule of three;

XXIX.

Preceded by addition and subtraction—
Multiplication and division too—
Follow'd by decimal and vulgar frcation,
Which brings at once all algebra to view.
And then the sciences of deep abstraction . . . . "
"Friend," quoth the monarch, "This will never do:
T' would take me all my life, sir . . . by the powers!
I want to learn the science in three hours."

XXX.

The sequel of the story, you all know :
 Indeed 't was almost too well known, to tell :
My purpose was, in telling it, to show
 How kings upon the shortest process dwell :
How, Presto ! they would to their object go :
 Just like a juggler with his cup and bell—
Without reflection, except now and then,
That nature, cannot be controll'd like men.

XXXI.

But if no king to learn the mathematics,
 A royal method in this world discovers,
It must be own'd, in marriage's erratic,
 The case is not the same with royal lovers :
The vulgar herd, need *time*, for Love's ecstatics—
 Long round the torch of Hymen Cupid hovers ;
The spider Love, his net around them spreads ;
And ever and anon they break the threads :

XXXII.

And then the spider on them darts afresh,
 And spins his cordage round them and around :
Till caught in Love's inextricable mesh,
 They break through all, in wedlock's fetters bound :
And this, with spirits not o'erclogg'd with flesh,
 A work of weeks, or months, or years is found—
Nay, sometimes they protract the blissful day,
Till their teeth fail them, and their hair turns gray.

XXXIII.

The vulgar, to be bound in wedlock's chains,
Need mutual passion and congenial age;
Assorted tempers, kindred joys and pains;
And hidden sympathies which love engage:
Esteem, which long and frequent converse gains;
Each other's faults to bear, and to assuage:
All this for lovers, even in their prime,
In progress slow must be the work of time.

XXXIV.

Not so, with kings—'t is all the same to them:
They sell their daughters, and they buy their wives:
To snuff the blossom, they observe the stem;
And seek for queens like bees within their hives—
A king, to find a matrimonial gem
His bargain foul, in open market drives:
A princely marriage, for convenience makes:
And then, a mistress for enjoyment takes.

XXXV.

Mac Morrogh thus, his daughter sold to Clare—
And scarcely had they once each other seen,
When they were coupled as a wedded pair
And priests were call'd, with aid to intervene:
A mitred bishop made the nuptial prayer;
A joyous banquet clos'd the night serene:
And there, his harp, a bard of Erin strung,
To strains of ecstasy, and thus he sung.

THE SONG.

Nought shines so bright in beauty's eyes,
As the bold warrior's gallant bearing:
The proudest deems his heart a prize;
The fairest would his fate be sharing;
Let Truth, let Valor be thy guide;
And faithful love, thy priceless jewel—
Thou ne'er shalt lack a lovely bride;
Nor find a female bosom cruel.

'T is true the soldier's life is short;
But what is life, depriv'd of action?
The craven coward's base resort;
A universe without attraction.
Then, urge thy courser to the field,
And thou shalt gain renown in story—
Compel the fiercest foe to yield;
Or die upon the bed of glory.

XXXVI

The song was partial—more of war than love:
For Dermot's heart, the wary harper knew,
Form'd of the vulture rather than the dove,
Would to his savage character be true.
His thoughts intent, all other things above,
On vengeance, and his country to subdue:
And Erin's bards were then, I grieve to say,
Loose moralists, as at the present day.

XXXVII.

And scarce three days the nuptial knot was tied,
When Dermot summon'd Strongbow to the field—
Thus lie the seeds of cruelty and pride
Within the germ of princely love conceal'd.
And Strongbow coldly left his blooming bride,
But swore his vows in heaven were all anneal'd,
And gentle Eva had resign'd her heart;
And bade him go, reluctant though to part.

XXXVIII.

And Dublin was the victim then selected;
Where Dermot's vengeance once had rag'd before:
Some secret movement there he had detected,
Of Erin's cause the standard to restore;
And all the people, deeply he suspected
Of disaffection, to say nothing more;
And so resolv'd, their favor to regain,
To sack the town, and heap her streets with slain.

XXXIX.

The king of Connaught, not till then aware
Of the dangers pending o'er the isle,
Had learnt the landing of the bands of Clare;
And then, the nuptials held in royal style:
His kingdom to defend was now his care;
From British robbers and from traitors vile:
O'er Erin's isle, the blast his trumpet blew;
And patriot thousands to his standard flew.

XL.

In loose array he march'd, the foe to meet;
His hasty levies shout, ERIN GO BRAGH!
Unpractic'd when to sally, when retreat,
Or distant bands in concert close to draw.
Aimless in victory, helpless in defeat,
And even restive to their chieftain's law:
Their swarming numbers only serve to tell;
And of the invader's host the triumph swell.

XLI.

In Dermot's and his ally Strongbow's host,
The hundreds, scarcely Roderick's thousands match'd,
But firm and marshall'd orders was their boast:
Each to his several station was attach'd.
To every leader was assign'd his post:
To all, the chieftains' order were despatch'd.
It seemed as if one breath inspired the whole;
A single body and a single soul.

XLII.

Milo de Cogan, a fierce English knight,
With a small troop of archers led the van:
And Donald, champion of his father's right,
Brought equal Irish numbers, man for man,
The center, Raymond marshall'd for the fight;
And Dermot there himself proclaim'd the ban—
Three hundred Welshmen follow'd Strongbow's spear;
And with one thousand Irish clos'd the rear.

XLIII.

Young Alexanders; you whose midnights pale
   Plod o'er Scott's Military Institute;
And find your labors of not much avail;
   From this last stanza may derive some fruit—
Here we may learn to mix, like rum and ale,
   The veteran soldier, with the raw recruit.
Till, in the pleasant compound will appear,
The fire of brandy and the froth of beer.

XLIV.

This compound Roderick's forces overaw'd,;
   With tenfold numbers, they dar'd never meet them—
And after some small skirmishes abroad,
   At once abandon'd all attempt to beat them.
Then home sickness, like rats the bosom gnaw'd,
   Of Roderick's levies, nor could he defeat them.
Home they all hied, to his severe bereavement,
And boasted there of many a bold achievement.

XLV.

Of this event it sickens me to tell—
   So dark a tarnish on so bright a cause:
But I must give the facts as they befel;
   And censure where I cannot yield applause—
They came their country's cruel foes to quell—
   To fight for Erin's freedom and her laws.
What shame to see them at the trial day,
Slink from her standard, dastardly away!

XLVI.

But let not Erin suffer in your mind ;
  If her brave children once were known to flee—
Consult Columbia's annals, you shall find
  The same with those who sought to make her free.
In sooth, militia-men you cannot bind,
  To serve for six months when engag'd for three—
Whence you may come to this conclusion just :
On raw militia not too much to trust.

XLVII.

There is, indeed, to speak without aspersion,
  Another way, but some, I know, will frown ;
To try them, by Court-martial for DESERTION,
  And hang them up at once, or shoot them down.
But I, to this must own some small aversion,
  Though much approv'd by chiefs of high renown.
And so to steer aloof from all contention,
Forbear to recommend this new invention.

XLVIII.

King Roderick had not nerve to bear him through
  A process quite so short and energetic ;
Nor needed afterwards hold up to view
  Wolves in sheep's clothing with complaint pathetic—
He saw in spite of all that he could do,
  Depart his patriots peripatetic.
Forc'd to retire within his own estate,
And leave devoted Dublin to her fate.

XLIX.

Devoted Dublin, to avert her fate,
By self defence was now, in no condition—
Fire had consum'd her only guarded gate;
She saw, her sole resource was in submission.
Her holy prelate, Lawrence, went too late,
To plead for pardon with sincere contrition—
For Dermot's fury, swelling to the flood;
Could be appeas'd by nothing less than blood.

L.

In fruitless parleys with the holy priest,
And captious cavilings, he bred delay;
Till the appointed time of truce had ceas'd,
And sent him then with barren words away:
Meantime the Britons, eager for their feast,
The city storm'd, and sack'd till close of day:
But from their grasp, her chieftain, Asculph, slips,
And from her port escapes, with thirty ships.

LI.

Enough of war and slaughter—for the Muse
To higher aims would bid her numbers flow—
Nor further yet to follow, would she choose
The still disgusting tale of human woe.
And Albion's Henry, learnt the news,
From the Welsh warrior of the potent bow;
Forbad, by proclamation, at that season,
All further deeds of arms, on pain of treason.

LII.

For Albion's monarch, with suspicious eye
The progress of his British bands had seen—
Mark'd the new purpose of his old ally
And bold pretentions, with inspection keen :
Saw Dermot's spirit now aspiring high,
Until it stirr'd his jealousy and spleen :
The humble suppliant of Aquitaine
Now claim'd o'er Erin's whole extent to reign.

LIII.

But this was not Plantagenet's design—
Of Adrian's grant HE never had lost sight—
Still deem'd it of authority divine,
Though now contesting with the pope his right :
A kneeling penitent at Becket's shrine ;
And threaten'd with an interdict outright :
Though Albion's realm he scarce could call his own,
He yet resolv'd to mount Ierne's throne.

LIV.

When Dermot his protection had implor'd,
And he to him his letters patent granted ;
To Leinster's lands he pray'd to be restor'd ;
His own domain was all that he had wanted.
But now, to loftier flights his projects soar'd,
For the whole Island his ambition panted.
But Henry vow'd to slide him on the shelf ;
And take the crown of Ireland for himself.

LV.

And soon, at Milford-haven he assembled
Four hundred transports and a royal fleet—
And slowly, with devotions well dissembled
O'er Cambrio's mountains, progress made complete
And Clare in Dublin, at his summons trembled;
And flew to join him, falling at his feet—
His favor by submission prompt retriev'd;
And homage vow'd for all his lands receiv'd.

LVI.

And, will the pious reader deem it odd,
That Henry, prostrate, and in humble prayer;
Now, at St. David's, in the house of God,
To ask the benizon of Heaven did dare?
'T is useless, o'er the ways of Heaven to plod
To man short-sighted they mysterious are:
But true religion views with indignation,
Of dark hypocrisy the profanation.

LVII.

At Waterford he landed from his fleet:
Strongbow, Fitz-Andelm, in his host enroll'd:
With Bohun, Lacy, and Fitz-Bernard meet,
Five hundred knights, four thousand archers bold:
Eager to gather fame by warlike feat
And counsellors to service train'd of old.
And having first, for safety, built a fort;
He held at Waterford, a royal court.

LVIII.

And then by proclamation he made known,
  That not for conquest, or for war he came;
But to take mere possession of his own,
  And his clear right on Erin's realm to claim.
Not clearer was his right to Albion's throne:
  Britons and Irish were to him the same.
He came o'er Erin to extend the laws;
And to promote religion's holy cause.

LIX.

The minor chieftains of Hibernia's land,
  Perceiv'd the helpless weakness of her shore;
And since the landing of Fitz-Stephen's band
  Saw they could trust her native strength no more.
Three gangs of British outlaws, feebly mann'd,
  Had spread their conquests half the island o'er:
And she in spite of all her king could do,
Had fail'd their paltry numbers to break through.

LX.

But now the monarch of the sister isle,
  A large and well appointed host had brought:
To him, submission would but change the style
  Of their possessions, with his sanction fraught—
To *him*, resistance, might excite a smile,
  But of success could scarce inspire the thought:
Nor could it be forgotten that his claim
Was consecrated by the pontiff's name.

LXI.

To his protection now they might resort,
Their lands, their goods, their persons to secure:
From his own vassals at his royal court,
Whose grasping talons they might else endure.
Henceforth, for forfeitures of any sort
The grants of Dermot could no more enure:
From the small robbers, happy was their fate,
To fly, at once, for refuge to the great.

LXII.

In crowds to Henry's standard they repair'd,
And paid their homage to the British lion.
Cork, Limerick, Ossory, the Decies shar'd
Macarthy, Donchad, O'Faolan, O'Brien,
With others, who their fealty declar'd
And stoop'd the tyrant's livery to try on.
And Henry promis'd from his gracious throne,
They still should hold possession of their own.

LXIII.

And Albion's king, by sharp experience taught,
Of holy church the favor to obtain;
With wary foresight, Cashel's prelate sought,
And made to him, his gracious purpose plain.
To mend the nation's morals was the thought
Which o'er them first had prompted him to reign;
And still his bosom glow'd with zeal intense,
To prop the church, and levy Peter's pence.

U of M

LXIV.

At Cashel now a synod was conven'd,
Of all the holy prelates of the land:
And not a sin or frailty could be glean'd,
But stood expos'd before that sacred band.
No crime was shelter'd, not a vice was screen'd,
Of all that call'd for the reforming hand:
And what the sins were, would the reader learn;
From the propos'd reforms he shall discern.

LXV.

First wedlock never must be solemniz'd,
Of kin within canonical degrees:
And children must *in public* be baptiz'd
And taught to know at least the church's fees.
And lands and tenements should be devis'd
To wives and children as the sire should please;
The dead, in church-yards only, buried be,
And all the church's lands from taxes free.

LXVI.

This, was the searching process of reform;
A precious model for all after times;
This was to justify invasion's storm,
And Strongbow's robberies, and Dermot's crimes.
One vice suppress'd, will sometimes breed a swarm,
As has been witness'd since, in other climes:
But when, O, when, did Conquest ever dare
Unveil her Gorgon face, with snakes so rare?

LXVII.

But while that holy synod thus disclos'd
  THEIR standard sense of piety and morals;
In strains of adulation they compos'd
  For Henry's head a verdant crown of laurels:
With steaming frankincense, his senses dos'd,
  Without inquiring into Becket's quarrels:
To him their lands and tenements convey'd:
And promis'd fealty, and homage paid.

LXVIII.

His gracious presence was alone ordain'd
  Of vicious ages past, to lay the storm:
And having from his royal hand obtain'd
  The matchless blessing of this great reform;
For them the further duty yet remain'd
  With Albion's church's rites their faith to warm.
And thus, redeem'd from wretchedness and sin;
The realm a new epocha must begin.

LXIX.

And Henry now to Dublin bends his course,
  In gorgeous and magnificent array;
Advancing at the head of all his force,
  In weary pomp and politic display;
His archers, knights and mailmen, foot and horse,
  In close attendance marshall'd him the way:
And all the princes of the region round
To join and swell his retinue were found.

LXX.

At Dublin, for the monarch there was rais'd
  Of wickerwork, a palace large and fair;
'Twas not a Louvre, but the work was prais'd;
  The courtiers thought it had a royal air:
And here the king the Irish lords amaz'd,
  With piles of massive silver, rich and rare;
With costly viands, music, wines and dress—
And all, a mighty monarch could possess.

LXXI.

And here, immers'd in mirth and jollity—
  He solemniz'd the Saviour's natal day:
With festal gambols of frivolity,
  So fascinating to the young and gay:
Politeness joining with his polity,
  Beguiling hours of idleness away;
Smoothing the rugged brows of Erin's race,
With courtly forms of elegance and grace

LXXII.

And thus the stormy days of winter past,
  In joyous revels, till returning bloom,
Brought with the breathing of the vernal blast,
  To Henry, tidings of far deeper gloom:
Pope Alexander, into fury cast,
  By the deep tragedy of Becket's doom;
Had sent his legates from his sacred side,
To try the king, and sink in dust his pride.

LXXIII.

Two priests, from Rome, deputed to inquire
  If Albion's king, in angry passion's flood,
Did with four subjects of his own conspire,
  And share the guilt of martyr'd Becket's blood!
In these days, should the pope depute a friar
  On such inquiry, he would quickly scud.
But *then* had Albion's king shown disobedience;
The pope had solv'd his subjects from allegience.

LXXIV.

The legates, Theodin and Albert nam'd,
  Before them summon'd Henry to appear;
But he, with spirit not entirely tam'd;
  Embark'd, to shun them, the preceeding year.
And now, with summons menacing they claim'd
  His presence, his full innocence to clear:
While o'er his head the scourge impending waves;
The threaten'd vengeance of THE SLAVE OF SLAVES.

LXXV.

And Henry thought it safer to comply,
  Than brave the venerated pontiff's power—
Though from his conquest he should seem to fly,
  When most his adverse fortune seem'd to lower.
Though his own vassals might perchance deny,
  He once withdrawn, the homage of an hour:
And Erin's sons, reminded of their fame,
Might rise, her former freedom to reclaim.

LXXVI.

From his new realm resolving to retire,
He summons all his vassal lords to meet;
Prescribes the measures which the times require,
And for the future guards against defeat.
With zeal for him their bosoms to inspire,
Grants as if Erin's conquest were complete;
And makes of Ulster, Meath, and Connaught cession,
As if his own already, by profession.

LXXVII.

But Roderick, king of Connaught, stood alone,
Aloof, and homage still refus'd to yield—
And on the banks of Shannon for his throne,
His faithful vassals brought into the field.
Too weak to meet the British force, his own
In self defence his royal right might shield—
And Henry's envoys parley'd, all in vain,
His vows of homage for their lord to gain.

LXXVIII.

And Ulster's princes by their distance too,
Encourag'd, to their independence clung;
And Henry had not leisure to subdue,
Or gain their vows of homage, old or young:
In arms, resistance he met not, 'tis true;
But on the wheel of Fortune, Conquest hung.
And ages pass'd, with Erin's sons untam'd;
Ere she as Albion's vassal could be claim'd.

LXXIX.

But Henry with his force from Dublin sail'd;
Return'd to Albion—thence to France repair'd;
Where to the pontiff's legates he detail'd,
That he in Becket's murder had not shar'd.
Inquiry further, little had avail'd
Amends to make, his purpose he declar'd;
And call'd the saintly relics to attest
That Becket's death had sorely griev'd his breast.

LXXX.

He promis'd, for requital of the loss,
To send two hundred knights for the crusade;
And should the pope require it, take the cross
Himself, and blessed Palestine invade—
And, deeming earthly kingdoms less than dross;
Would cause the pontiff's will to be obey'd:
Confessing that his hold on Albion's throne,
Was at the holy pontiff's will alone.

LXXXI.

And now the priestly legates in their turn
Absolve the royal penitent from guilt:
No more the holy pontiff's bowels yearn
For vengeance on the blood of Becket spilt
Profuse, his gracious favor, in return
Confirms the deed, on fraud and falsehood built:
And grants what Adrian had bestow'd before;
THE RIGHT SUPREME TO ERIN'S VERDANT SHORE.

LXXXII.

Thus was the shame of servitude her lot:
  And has been since, from that detested day,
When Dermot all his country's claims forgot,
  And basely barter'd all her rights away.
Oh! could the Muse be heard, his name should rot
  In fresh, immortal, unconsum'd decay—
And be with Arnold's name transmitted down,
First in the roll of infamous renown.

LXXXIII.

Nor was the hand of vengeful justice slow,
  In retribution on his head to fall—
For death's relentless hand had laid him low,
  Ere he could answer Henry's sovereign call.
From dreams of empire, form'd in fancy's glow
  He now awoke: his hopes were blasted all—
And conscience whisper'd with envenom'd tongue,
That all his tortures from himself had sprung.

LXXXIV.

He first with daring and relentless hand
  Had torn of friendship and of love the ties—
Had rent, of wedlock's sacred vows the band,
  And taken fraud and falsehood for allies:
Expell'd with justice from his native land,
  To Albion's tyrant for revenge he flies;
Betrays his trust, pays homage for his throne;
And seals his country's ruin with his own.

LXXXV.

When first the royal summons met his eye,
  To come and homage to his lord renew :
The task, phosphoric pencils might defy
  To paint the storm, it o'er his visage threw :
Pride, envy, hatred, disappointment vie
  In his rack'd soul, each other to subdue.
Yet to his breast with wild commotion toss'd,
Rung in one chime, that all for him was lost.

LXXXVI.

And now concentrated, burst forth his rage :
  He curst the day on which he had been born ;
For, on the record of his life, no page
  Could speak of comfort to his state forlorn—
No cordial drop of memory to assuage
  Of fell remorse the vital-searching thorn :
A burning fever seized on every vein,
[illegible] mortal madness fasten'd on his brain.

LXXXVII.

And to his wilder'd senses, Erin's saints
  Appear with lighted torches in their hands,
Applying scorpion scourges till he faints,
  And then reviving him, with blazing brands ;
While o'er his head a frowning Fury paints
  In letters which he reads and understands—
" Expect no mercy from thy Maker's hand !
THOU HADST NO MERCY ON THY NATIVE LAND."

LXXXVIII.

And to the shades the indignant spirit fled,
And THUS was Erin's conquest first achiev'd;
THUS Albion's monarch first became her head:
And now her freedom shall be soon retriev'd.
For, (mark the Muse, if rightly she has read,
Let this her voice prophetic be believ'd.)
Soon, soon, shall dawn the day, as dawn it must,
When Erin's sceptre, shall be Erin's trust.

LXXXIX.

And here I hang my harp upon the willow;
And will no longer importune the Muse;
Nor woo her nightly visits to my pillow;
Nor more implore her favor or abuse.
Brave sons of Erin, o'er the Atlantic billow!
The harp is yours! will you to hear refuse?
Take, take it back—yourselves the strain prolong;
And give your Dermot's name to deathless song.

XC.

For, ho! if ever on the roll of Time
Since man has on this blessed planet dwelt,
A soul existed saturate with crime,
Or the deep curse of after ages felt;
Yours was his country, Erin was his clime;
Nor yet, has justice with his name been dealt.
My voice, alas! is weak and cannot sing—
Touch, touch yourselves the never-dying string.

www.ingramcontent.com/pod-product-compliance
Lightning Source LLC
LaVergne TN
LVHW021430110826
845150LV00007B/2170